MEAN JOE GREENE

AND THE STEELERS' FRONT FOUR

MEAN JOE GREENE AND THE STEELERS' FRONT FOUR

by Larry Fox

Introduction by Chuck Noll,
Head Coach of the Pittsburgh Steelers

ILLUSTRATED WITH PHOTOGRAPHS

DODD, MEAD & COMPANY
NEW YORK

Library of Congress Cataloging in Publication Data
Fox, Larry.
   Mean Joe Greene and the Steelers' front four.

   1. Greene, Joe.   2.   Pittsburgh Steelers (Football
Club)   I. Title.
GV939.G74F69   796.33'2'0924   75-29211
ISBN 0-396-07203-8

To Art Rooney and the Pittsburgh organization
for demonstrating that success and humanity
are not necessarily incompatible, and to four
guys who can teach a lesson to us all

Acknowledgments

First and most of all, thanks to Joe Gordon of the Steelers' publicity staff, who threw open the doors of his office and his amazing files and made it possible for me to see all the people I had to see. Also to Art Rooney, who not only provided his time but also sets the tone for this most cooperative of organizations. The front four themselves—Joe Greene, Dwight White, L. C. Greenwood, and Ernie Holmes—were extremely gracious and cooperative. Also thanks to Chuck Noll for his insights and fine introduction, and to George Perles, Dan Radakovich, Ralph Berlin, Ed Kiely, Dan Rooney, Art Rooney, Jr., Bill Nunn, John Brown, Bob Fry, John Dockery, Spider Lockhart, Bob Sprenger of the Kansas City Chiefs and that city's fine 101 Committee, and Joe Browne of the NFL office.

Contents

Introduction

CHUCK NOLL

Head Coach, Pittsburgh Steelers

It's a funny thing in this business. You set your goals, you work like hell to get there . . . and as soon as you've achieved them, you turn around and reset those goals. You forget about what's gone in the past. We tell our football players that it's the getting there that's worthwhile and that's what has to be the reward. Once you think you've "arrived," you're over the hill.

So, in a way, I'm reluctant to talk about the past and what our football team accomplished in 1974. We got to a plateau, but we want to go higher.

However, what we've done can help us in the future. The players now know what they can accomplish when they work as a team, together. You talk about four guys and they do provide a leadership thrust, but it takes every individual on a football team. We won a Super Bowl because we had forty-seven guys playing well and carrying their share. Now I think we've got the message. The horizons are unlimited when you work as a group, and that's probably the biggest thing that happened to our football team in 1974.

These four guys—Joe Greene, Dwight White, Ernie Holmes, and L. C. Greenwood—are competitors as well as buddies, you know. They compete like hell with one another, in fact, and this often makes things very lively. Each of them has a great desire to get to the ball and to the passer, and they don't want anyone else to do it. When you have that kind of feeling on your defensive unit, you know you're going to get the job done. The guys pulling together becomes very much a leadership factor, and that's something I'd never seen before from an entire unit like our defensive line. And from respect comes friendship.

The biggest thing they showed was a refusal-to-be-denied attitude. There are a lot of things that can happen to a team when it wants something very badly and then somebody fouls up. It can be an official, another player, a fumble by the offense. Take the Oakland game for the AFC championship, the game that got us into the Super Bowl. Our offense was down there many times early but did not score. We missed a field goal, had a pass intercepted. Things like this can upset a defense, especially an emotional defense that wants it very badly. Our defense did not get upset.

Whatever was written in the newspapers during the season, they could care less. You could say whatever you wanted about our team but nothing took away our concentration. It was really locking in on an objective, and I've never seen it displayed quite like it was by this football team, especially by the defensive line. It's something you had to observe to appreciate.

Everybody could have become more involved in our quarterback situation than in getting ready to play the game, but instead everybody zeroed in on his own job. They didn't worry about what the hell was happening here or happening there, and that's the thing that really made it work.

In the Super Bowl, all we asked was that our defensive line play up to its ability. That's all we've ever asked of them. But, of course, we think they happen to have pretty exceptional ability, and so that enables us to set our goals fairly high.

To achieve those goals in the Super Bowl, we had to get leadership from our front four and then we had to get forty-seven guys working together. We did, and the sum total was really great. Those guys really carried out their jobs to the nth degree; stopping the run, rushing the passer. Our defense was fantastic.

You get leadership in a lot of ways. Actually, everybody leads, either positively or negatively. But you lead by doing, not by word of mouth. When I first came to Pittsburgh, we had leadership by mouth and not by action. That kind of stuff lasts about two minutes. Everybody's talking when you get to the stadium and you get all emotionally riled up. Then you go out on the field and the other guy knocks you on your tail and it's gone. It has to be leadership by action, and that's what those guys up front have given us.

When you start putting a defense together up front, it's important that you have people who are factors, people with whom the offense has to concern itself and who force the opponent to change his normal pattern. You have to make them say, "Our man can't handle this guy," and start doubling up on the blocking. We have that kind of people.

You start with Joe Greene, the first player I drafted when I came to Pittsburgh. I had scouted him personally in college and I had never seen anybody block him one-on-one. With his great quickness, speed, and strength, he has pretty much everything you're looking for. With L. C. Greenwood, you have quickness and speed. Our whole front four has the ability to find and get to the ball, but in this L. C. probably leads.

In Ernie Holmes and Dwight White we have guys with great strength. Ernie has unreal strength. He's what we call a head-butter. He can destroy a blocker. Dwight has all of that and he's a fine pass rusher. Their styles complement each other.

The problem, of course, is maintaining all this. You have to keep that emotional edge. You have to remember what got you there, the prices you had to pay. You have to be willing to pay the same price again.

The thing about this business is that you're always remembered by the last game you played, which is fine. It keeps you from sitting around on your butt. It makes you do what you have to do.

1

"I May Die on That Field"

Dwight White felt lousy. The rest of the Pittsburgh Steelers were relaxed and happy as their chartered jet droned through the evening skies to New Orleans, where they would set up camp to prepare for the Super Bowl, one week ahead. But Dwight White had little to say.

The Steelers had been a loose group through most of the season as they struggled to the American Football Conference championship. Dwight White, their right defensive end, was the most ebullient of them all.

The nickname White brought to the Steelers from college was Mad Dog, in honor of his play on the field. Out of uniform, though, a more appropriate description would have been Motor Mouth. Dwight seldom stopped talking. But on this flight he sat quietly, hunched down in his seat.

Dan Rooney, vice-president and general manager of the Steelers, noticed that White was not participating in his teammates' ribaldry during most of the two-and-a-half hour trip. Rooney was concerned.

White's conversational patter was an important barometer

1

for judging the mood of this team. He was also a key member
of the most important single unit on the Steelers, the defensive line, or front four, which had been dubbed by some "The
Steel Curtain." L. C. Greenwood played the other end and
the tackles were Ernie Holmes and Joe Greene.

Greene, known as Mean Joe Greene but actually a sensitive soul, a gentle giant, according to teammates, was the most
celebrated of the four, the best player, the leader. Greenwood, known as Hollywood Bags (supposedly because he kept
his bags packed awaiting a call from Hollywood to become a
movie star), outwardly was the most flamboyant. But his
gaudy outfits, gold football shoes, and ultracool demeanor
actually hid a rather shy personality. He rarely spoke up in
the huddle. He and Greene had been drafted in the same
year, 1969, Joe in the first round, L. C. in the tenth. Greene
had become an instant star but it took Greenwood longer to
blossom. Once Greenwood became established, he may have
resented Greene's dominance and salary, and so, in quest of
at least monetary satisfaction, he had signed to jump to Birmingham of the new World Football League the next season.
His teammates then began to call him Birmingham Bags, but
the swift and slender Mississippian responded with his most
spectacular season.

White and Holmes had come along two years after the
others. White made it as a starter right away, but Holmes
had to spend humiliating time on the taxi squad. He was the
strongest of the four and the least stable. Two years earlier
he had suffered a nervous breakdown and had been involved
in a shooting incident that almost landed him in jail. He recovered from that setback to enjoy his best season as a pro in
1973. Some said he played better than Greene that year, and

he seemed to think so too. In an effort to establish a public identity, he had taken to trimming his hair in the shape of an arrow. The ploy worked. He got a lot of interviews and his teammates sometimes called him Arrowhead. But mostly the 260-pounder was known as Fats, because he had weighed over 300 in college. He seemed to need the identification of being a team member more than the others.

These four men, so different in personality, had much in common besides their position down in the pit of pro football combat. All four are black and roughly the same age, their late twenties. All come from the same general area. White, Holmes, and Greene all grew up in Texas and went to college in that state. (White was born in Hampton, Virginia, but his parents were native Texans and had moved back when Dwight was in his early teens.) Greenwood, from Mississippi, attended Arkansas AM&N, close enough to Texas so they had all been scouted by the same man, the late Jess Thompson.

Because of this common background, the four had developed a unity rare in professional sports, where it is not unusual for two men to play side by side for years and never visit each other's home. These four had become soul brothers in the best sense of the term.

"We're just a good combination of personalities, abilities, ambition, and intelligence," White explained one day after the season. "All four of us come from basically the same background. Since we went to all-black schools, our high school experiences were the same. This extended to our family lives, living in the ghetto, where you had to work, had to get up and get it for yourself. We all happen to have met at the same point, in the utopia of pro football, but a lot of the

ways we think now are influenced by the way we were then.
That's why we all seem to think the same way."

Like the Corsican brothers in the old movie that appears
occasionally on the late show, when one of the four hurt,
physically or emotionally, the others winced in distress.

In a season not without turmoil as the coaches shifted the
main leadership job among three quarterbacks, this front
four provided an anchor of stability. Since one of the quarterbacks was black (Joe Gilliam) and the job eventually was
taken from him and returned to a blond white southerner
from small-town Louisiana (Terry Bradshaw), the front four
could have helped tear the team apart. They did not. Instead, they were a major influence in holding the Steelers on
course.

That's why Dan Rooney, capable oldest son of the team's
owner, was concerned when he noticed Dwight White
wrapped in silence on the flight down to New Orleans, his
sharp intelligent wit apparently sheathed for the trip. What
in the world is this? Rooney thought. Don't tell me Dwight's
getting up tight already about this game.

"They've all got their thing," a teammate had once said
about the front four. "Joe is just Joe, he's got his great
ability. L. C. is supercool, and Ernie has the haircut. Dwight's
thing is conversation."

Rooney knew that if White were overwhelmed by the importance of the Steelers' first Super Bowl appearance in history, it would not bode well for the entire team's approach.
Most teams choked in their first Super Bowl appearance.
Minnesota, Pittsburgh's opponent, already had played twice
in the National Football League's climax game. This experience could prove a major advantage, especially if the Steelers

reacted negatively to the pressure. Given the closeness of the front four, the Steelers' dominant force, Rooney worried whether White's apparent tightness might be catching.

As it turned out, it wasn't the contagiousness of White's mental attitude that Rooney had to worry about.

White had been suffering from a head cold the last month of the season; just the sniffles, he thought, but the tension of the final weeks had kept him from sleeping well. He began to need sleeping pills just to get his rest. And then there was the abrupt change in climate as the Steelers flew out to Oakland for their AFC championship game victory over the Raiders, and then back to Pittsburgh.

Late the next week, White began to have back pains, which he attributed to some unnoticed blow during the game. He often had these muscle spasms during a season, but usually a little heat treatment cured them. On the flight to New Orleans the pain was recurring. Dwight sought out trainer Ralph Berlin for a medicated heating plaster that he could tape to his back. The pain worsened, but White went ahead with plans to visit the French Quarter with Joe Greene after they had checked into the hotel. They would have dinner and a few drinks. (L. C. Greenwood and Ron Shanklin, a wide receiver, were to follow in another car, but they got separated and ended up at a different restaurant.)

Down on Bourbon Street, White and Greene did the scene, ate some seafood, drank some beer, listened to some jazz, looking for all the world like a couple of typical 260-pound tourists. But Dwight's back was paining him more and more. There were knifelike jabs every time he shifted his body. "Hey, I got to go," he finally muttered to Greene. At first Joe tried to jolly White out of it, but then he realized his friend was really sick.

Dwight was driving, and he was just barely able to ease his body under the wheel. It was agony just to turn the ignition key. But somehow White managed the twenty-minute drive back to the team's Fontainebleu Hotel headquarters. They got there just in time. In the lobby, White says, "It really hit me." He doubled over in pain and sweat poured off his body. Greene helped him to his room.

White will never forget that frightening moment. "My body was twisted over and it hurt me just to breathe. I thought I was going to die."

What made it worse was that White had never been seriously ill before. "I was going to try to do this life here without ever being sick, but I guess I've blown it," he jokes today.

Steve Davis, White's roommate, was out. The team doctor was staying at another hotel. Coach Chuck Noll, traveling secretary Jim Boston, and Dan Rooney had gone to dinner. Greene finally roused trainer Ralph Berlin, who came running with his assistant, Bob Milie.

Berlin immediately realized that White needed hospital treatment. But where to go? They had just arrived in a strange city; it was almost like being in a foreign country. The NFL undoubtedly had made hospital arrangements for the visiting teams, but the men who would know where had gone to dinner. A security guard had been posted near the players' rooms to keep them from being harassed. "Where's the nearest hospital?" Berlin asked him.

"Charity Hospital," the guard replied, and he gave directions on how to get there. Milie got the station wagon as

Greene and Berlin helped White—still literally doubled over like an inverted "L"—onto the service elevator.

Charity Hospital turned out to be just that, a ghetto area clinic. The emergency room staff said Saturday night had been worse, but Berlin couldn't imagine how. At 11 P.M. this Sunday, the waiting room and halls were crowded with weekend casualties. There were drunks who had fallen downstairs, survivors of bloody car wrecks, and victims of fights and stabbings. Berlin had served with the Marines in Korea. The scene reminded him of a front-line aide station.

White was just another casualty as nurses and interns bustled back and forth to tend the seriously wounded. Occasionally a nurse would marvel at White's size and build. At 6'4", 255, he's an impressive man. Berlin, realizing they had come to the wrong place, fretted and tried to get someone on the phone. Anger and frustration began to boil in Joe Greene. "Those damn nurses saying, 'Oh, he's big,' and trippin' over his size when a man is hurt," Greene recalls, still angry over the delay. Finally one hapless intern wandered into range and Greene grabbed him as he would a quarterback trying to scramble for a first down. "I want something done *now!*" he bellowed, and at 6'4", 275 pounds, the bearded lineman can be a most impressive figure.

As if by magic, a resident physician appeared and the staff began to take some preliminary action. X rays and blood tests were ordered. But, although the hospital did its best, it really lacked the facilities and the staff for the kind of treatment White required. And once they were aware of who this patient was, they understandably hesitated to take major action.

By now it was past midnight. Milie and Greene returned

to the hotel, where they found Rooney and Boston just checking in after dinner. The two executives drove back to Charity Hospital and got hold of a team physician, Dr. John M. Best. Only then did they learn that arrangements had been made to take their players to Southern Baptist Hospital, a private institution. A transfer was quickly arranged.

Fearful now that he would not be able to play in the climactic game of his career the following Sunday, White called Dan Rooney to his bedside. "Get me out of here," he whispered.

Rooney put him off. "Just stay overnight so we can be sure you're okay," he said soothingly, as if speaking to one of his nine children.

Meanwhile, back at the hotel, Chuck Noll was getting a cryptic call from the front desk: "One of your players is in the hospital."

Tests the next morning showed that White's problem was more than a back spasm. It was pleurisy and viral pneumonia, serious illnesses. The doctors knew they had a week to get him ready, but only the other players were optimistic. "Dwight's a real critter. He'll come back," Greene predicted.

The hoop-la of Super Bowl Week formally begins on Monday, picture day, and both teams are required to be on the scene in game uniform. They pose for pictures, naturally, and stand for interviews. Tuesday, Wednesday, and Thursday they are also made available around the lunch hour in the most concentrated press coverage this side of the White House. The scene was totally unlike anything the Steelers had ever experienced, which is why first-time starters have such a hard time winning. Some coaches fight the circus and their anxiety is reflected by the players.

But Noll had been through a Super Bowl scene once before as an assistant to the Baltimore Colts when they were upset by the New York Jets. The Jets and Joe Namath, he remembered, had been superloose before that game. Noll warned his players to expect "a carnival atmosphere." His advice: "Relax and enjoy it. Too many people don't get the chance to be here."

The Steelers followed his advice to the extreme. They seemed almost manic in their looseness, and on picture day it seemed half of them showed up with their own cameras, and posed more for each other than for the press. Noll joked later in the week that the Steelers were the first team in Super Bowl history to intimidate the press, yelling at them, "Come back! Come back!" when the formal interview period was over. The Steelers were unfailingly good-humored all week.

It was during the Monday picture session that Joe Greene became poignantly aware that the team was not complete. The players line up for an official squad picture "and that's when it dawned on me, Dwight wasn't there," Greene recalls. His distress was obvious when Holmes asked Joe about their missing teammate. Joe Greene puts great store in such formalities as team pictures. He still bristles when he recalls how L. C. Greenwood missed an appointment for a shot of the front four during the season. "It was such an insignificant thing, probably nobody else noticed it, but it really teed me off. You see, we're a group," Greene explained months later.

A large crowd surrounded Greene. He talked about what playing in this game meant and the mystique of the Super Bowl victory ring. "You can't take that ring away and that's what it's all about," he rumbled softly. "Money goes. You can go to the bank and borrow money, but you can't go to the bank and borrow a Super Bowl ring. That ring is like a crown and, not to boast, we're gonna get it."

Greene talked about playing against Ed White, the Vikings' best guard, a powerful figure. "He's so strong, there's no way I can hurt him head-to-head. I'm gonna use a cape, like a bullfighter," Joe laughed. He talked about chasing Fran Tarkenton, the Vikings' nimble quarterback. "I've never caught him yet. Has he slowed down?" he asked a reporter from Minnesota.

"We've got our work cut out for us, just like last week, but don't think we gave it all up in Oakland," Greene warned, referring to the previous week's emotional victory over the Raiders, perhaps Pittsburgh's most bitter rival.

In another section of the Tulane Stadium field, where the Steelers would practice and the game was to be played, L. C. Greenwood was answering questions. He would face the Vikings' best offensive lineman, tackle Ron Yary. Yary and Ed White played side by side on the right side of the Minnesota line. They spearheaded the Viking attack. L. C. and Greene would get most of the action.

"It's a challenge, and I like a challenge. I like to go out and play the best, and the side I'm on it looks as if I'll catch the heat every time," Greenwood drawled.

L. C., oldest of nine children who had ordered tickets for twenty-five friends and relatives from neighboring Mississippi, also faced a major task on the pass rush. Tarkenton liked to roll out to his right before passing. L. C.'s job would be to contain him, to "make him pull up so the pursuit can catch him or so he has to throw before he wants to." But if he came too fast, L. C. knew Tarkenton was still capable of scrambling around him.

Playing out his option to set up the jump to Birmingham (or another NFL team), Greenwood was very much aware that this could be his last game in a Steeler uniform. He was glad his finale would be in an appropriate showcase. It wouldn't be fitting for Hollywood Bags to depart in anything less than the Super Bowl. Catfish Hunter, the baseball pitcher, had just become a free agent and had signed for more than $3 million with the New York Yankees during the previous week. "Just call me Catfish Greenwood," joked L. C., who was aware also that the was becoming a free agent after a superlative season.

Greenwood turned briefly solemn when asked about the front four and the effect of White's absence. "It's a helluva thing to be on a team with three guys like that up front, guys you can work with and not worry about a thing," he said. "We're a unit, a team within a team. It's as if one-fourth of that team has been cut out."

Greenwood's eyes were hidden by sun glasses, but they had to be twinkling as he discussed the front four's social togetherness. He and White are bachelors, Holmes is divorced. "Joe is married, but his wife is not there much of the time, so we have a nice social life together. Since most of us are not married, we have a lot of time to go out at night," he said with a wide grin.

A guy in the crowd suggested they be known as the Bachelors III Plus One, a play on the name of swinging Joe Namath's bar.

Ernie Holmes and his haircut also drew a crowd, which was the general idea. "Before every game of the season I've had it trimmed. The hair is always ready," Holmes said. "I missed one game, against the Saints down here, with a virus, but ever since then I've been hitting people upside the head and enjoying it."

During the season, the Saints had replaced Milt Sunde at left guard with Andy Maurer, a younger man who had been traded away by Atlanta Falcon coach Norm Van Brocklin in a fit of pique during the players' strike that summer. Since Van Brocklin got fired and Maurer was in the Super Bowl, the blond lineman had a lot to laugh about, except maybe for the prospect of playing against Holmes. Holmes is a punishing defender who uses his head, according to one teammate, "like one of those iron balls they use to knock down buildings."

Holmes had said that if Sunde started, "since he's an old pro and knows a lot of tricks, I'll use a lot of tricks on him."

However, if the choice, as expected, was Maurer, "then I'll manhandle him more, use brute strength. I'll snatch him off the ground. It always helps my ego to snatch a two-hundred-and-eighty-pound guard off the ground."

Maurer, actually closer to 245, reacted with some annoyance to Holmes's threat. "I've been reading his crap all over the West and I'm real proud of him," he said sarcastically. "If he wants to talk like that, fine. I'm not a talker, I'm a doer." Still, he called Holmes an "underrated tackle" and said Ernie would be a cinch all-pro if it weren't for the shadow of Joe Greene next to him.

At the photo session little attention was being paid to Steve Furness, the Steelers' first substitute lineman at all four positions. The Steelers still considered White's illness not very serious. Official word that it was not a muscle spasm didn't reach the field until the players were beginning to disperse.

Regardless, they still thought Dwight would be out of the hospital momentarily.

Some Steeler watchers speculated that White actually was the lineman whose absence would hurt least. His season, while a good one, had been the least spectacular of the four. Besides, the Vikings were such a right-handed team that White's position didn't figure to be the point of attack. He would have been missed much more, for instance, against Oakland the game before. Oakland, with a southpaw quarterback in Ken Stabler and its top blockers on the left side of the line, is a left-handed team.

Furness, who had filled in well the day Holmes was sick in New Orleans, is basically a tackle. There was some speculation that the swifter Joe Greene might be moved out to end. However, when it came time to consider these alternatives, Chuck Noll elected to keep Greene where he was and take his chances with Furness at end. That way only one position would be weakened, not two.

Meanwhile, a team of physicians headed by Dr. David S. Huber of the Steelers and Dr. Charles Brown of the Saints worked overtime on Dwight White. (Both doctors are internists. Most football teams also have an orthopedic specialist who is usually more famous because he does the knee operations.) White was given inhalation treatments three times a day to try to clear his lungs and massive doses of antibiotics to fight the infection. For three days he lay in the hospital, weak and drugged. He slept virtually the entire day through, eating little. His weight dropped eighteen pounds. He lost muscle tone.

On Thursday, Dwight was released from the hospital in time to join the Steelers for their early-afternoon workout. Most of the pain was gone, but he felt weak and awkward. His equipment didn't seem to fit, like the first day of training camp, only worse. Just changing into his suit seemed to drain him of energy. He grew dizzy and almost fell out after trying to jog a lap or two.

Art Rooney, Dan's father and owner of the Steelers, had arrived in New Orleans that day. He always uses both the lineman's names in addressing White, a little private joke, and he was shocked when he saw Dwight's condition as he sat in the clubhouse after the aborted workout. "Gee, what's wrong?" Rooney blurted in genuine concern. He knew White had been sick, but all the reports out of New Orleans had been optimistic.

"You look awful," Rooney said. "You look as white as a . . . Dwight White!" At least White's sense of humor hadn't been lost along with the eighteen pounds. He started to laugh. It was his only laugh of the week.

After the workout, White stopped at the hospital for treatment and then returned to the hotel. But he had overdone it. As the night turned chilly, the pain in his chest returned. Dr. Huber came by and gave him something for the pain so he could sleep. The next morning Dwight was readmitted to Southern Baptist.

"You'd better get Furness ready. There's no way Dwight is going to play," the doctors told Noll.

En route to the hospital, they gave White the same message, but he vowed, "I'm going to play," and made a deal with the doctors. He would go peacefully back into the hospital if they would promise to let him out on game day and at least dress and watch from the sidelines. "Sure, sure," they agreed.

It was determination that had enabled White to survive

his teens in a Dallas ghetto and determination that had helped him overcome a near-crippling knee injury in college. He now knew what he required to get ready to play. Lack of food had weakened him as much as the infection during his first stay in the hospital. This time he would stuff down every bit of nourishment he could. Though he gagged on the food and had no taste for it, he forced himself to eat. The dramatic medical treatments continued.

Friday night White talked on the phone with George Perles, the defensive line coach. "I hear I'm not going to play on Sunday," White began.

"Yes, that's right," Perles replied honestly. "The doctor told me Thursday when you were on the field that you don't have a chance and to get Furness ready."

White again reacted angrily. "Look, George, I've worked all my life for this game and I'm going to play if at all possible."

Perles understood. "Dwight, if you are dressed for the game and if you are on the field and if you can go, you will play. If you're ready, you'll play," he promised.

"These people want me to lay on that bed, but I'm going to walk out; I'm not going to lay on that damned bed," White answered, and late Saturday night Dwight White rejoined his teammates at the hotel.

By this time the married players' wives had come down to join their husbands, and this required some reshuffling of roommates. Greenwood and White, bachelors, found themselves together. "If I feel the way I do now, there's no way I can play, but at least I want to be introduced," White told his new roomie.

"Well, make the entrance, and if you don't feel up to it,

come on out," Greenwood suggested. "There's no sense going out there and trying to do it when you know you can't, because there's somebody behind you who can carry the load."

Greenwood then left so White could get some sleep, and when L. C. awoke the next morning, White was already dressed. "Well, I may die on that field or they may have to stretcher me off, but I'm gonna play," White announced to his sleep-fogged roommate.

In the lobby, old Art Rooney asked him how he felt. "Well, I feel a lot better than I have before a lot of games that I've played," Dwight replied, but he was lying. He felt terrible.

Out at the stadium, a chill rain was just beginning to slack off. It was a good day to catch pneumonia, not get rid of it, but White slowly went about the business of pulling on his uniform and adjusting the heavy pads.

The doctors had told him he could dress, but they didn't think much of the idea of his warming up with the team. "But I gotta be with the team," he pleaded, and they grudgingly agreed. Now they admit they all expected White to go through light warmups and then fall out. Why argue with the guy and get him upset? He felt bad enough as it was. Furness was ready to go and the team and coaches had confidence in the third-year pro from Rhode Island.

Surprising everyone, although he did take it easy, White got through the warmups. Once again he sidled over to the doctors. "Can I start?" he begged. Dr. Huber obviously didn't want to be the man who broke Dwight White's heart. Besides, he would be watching Dwight closely. Fatigue probably would get White out of the game before any real damage was done, and if he was too weak to stop the Vikings, the coaches would lift him in a hurry. They'd be watching closely as well.

"Let me just play a couple of plays," White pleaded, sounding like the little boy who wants to stay up to watch television. "Well, okay," the doctor conceded, "but I'm going to watch you, and the first thing wrong that I notice, out you come and no arguments."

White agreed to the condition, but deep inside he still felt a flicker of doubt. He seemed to be feeling fine now. But was it just the excitement of the moment? The old adrenalin? Was he deluding himself to the extent that he might hurt the team? He sought out Joe Greene just before they went off the field. Greene knew what he wanted, and the two behemoths squared off and smashed full tilt into each other.

It was, said George Perles, who was watching, "a game hit, a head-knocker."

Ten yards away, Chuck Noll heard the crash, and his head snapped around. He saw what had happened and perhaps he allowed himself one of his tight little smiles.

Dwight White was ready, at least for the first series of downs. When the Pittsburgh Steelers went out to play Minnesota for the world's championship of professional football, the heart of their team, the team within a team, would be there: L. C. Greenwood, number 68; Joe Greene, number 75; Ernie Holmes, number 63 . . . and Dwight White, number 78.

2

"My Friends Call Me Joe"

Looking back, the Steeler family, which pretty much includes all of Pittsburgh, agrees that the team took its first step toward the Super Bowl by drafting Joe Greene out of North Texas State in 1969.

Greene is the man that Art Rooney, Jr., head of Steeler scouting, calls the "catalyst, the force that turned our team around."

Not that Greene was the first all-pro ever to wear a Pittsburgh uniform. There were many of his stature before, but they had been condemned to pursue their labors in an atmosphere of frustration and defeat. They, too, might have been catalysts if mixed with the proper ingredients.

For Greene to have the impact he did, the Steelers first had to make the commitment to introduce professionalism and efficiency into what had been a family-run old-crony hobby. Then they had to hire a coach to make it work, which they did only days before that 1969 draft in the person of young Chuck Noll.

Without Noll, whose will and determination were immediately put to the test, Mean Joe Greene might never have become a Steeler.

Here's the full story:

When the Steelers and their new coach first sat down to discuss the upcoming draft, strong consideration was given to selecting a quarterback. The team needed one, that's for sure, since slow-footed Dick Shiner was the incumbent. As they looked over the list of available seniors, they discovered a dandy. Terry Hanratty, from nearby Butler, Pennsylvania, was coming out of Notre Dame.

It was a perfect combination. Local boy comes home as Notre Dame hero to rescue Steelers. Sure, a lad named Hanratty playing for the Rooneys? It would sell a million tickets, and Hanratty's college credentials against the tough Notre Dame schedule were certainly acceptable.

On the negative side, however, Hanratty was coming off knee surgery, scouts inside pro football generally agreed his arm was not the strongest . . . and Noll had somebody else he wanted to pick.

Noll had been acquired off the staff of the Baltimore Colts, which afforded him two particular insights as he approached the draft. For one thing, the Colts the season before had played the Steelers and beaten them, 41–7. He knew they needed quality players up and down the line . . . and in the backfield, too. "Anyplace we get a good football player we'll be helping ourselves," he said.

Secondly, the Colts' college scouting setup gave the assistant coaches a very important role. Every spring they would be sent out to tour the campuses and look at prospects in person. The Colts split the country into sections, and Noll's area included Texas. Denton, Texas, a small town about thirty miles northwest of Dallas was the home of North Texas State College where Joe Greene succeeded in making a rather large impression on Chuck Noll.

Noll watched Greene in spring practice for three years, and when the team was in class, he would study films of their games. He liked Greene's size, strength, and speed, and especially the way he coiled his body and exploded off the ball at the center snap. There was one negative that appeared off and on in Greene's dossier. Scouts noted a tendency to "dog it," not to go all out on every play. But Noll had talked to Greene. He knew the young man's determination to play professional football. Put in competition he couldn't automatically dominate, Greene would be forced to play up to his capabilities on every down.

At those early Pittsburgh staff meetings, there was talk of picking a quarterback. "I don't think we can afford to take one," Noll interjected. "We need too much help in other areas."

He explained that "your supporting cast does it for a quarterback, and without a supporting cast your quarterback isn't going to be worth a darn anyway."

As an example, he pointed to Earl Morrall, a much-traveled veteran who had served without particular distinction in several NFL communities—including Pittsburgh—until he was traded to Baltimore. There he had just come off the bench for an injured Johnny Unitas to lead the Colts into the Super Bowl.

Noll said he felt Greene fell in the class of a Bob Lilly, Gino Marchetti, or Gene Brito as the rock about whom a defensive line, an entire defense, could be built. "I had covered Greene for about three years and felt he was an outstanding defensive

lineman. He fell into the category of someone the offense has
to give special attention to. I wanted someone like that on our
football team," he says today.

The Steelers, coming off a 2–11–1 season, had the fourth
selection in the draft, following Buffalo, Atlanta, and Philadelphia. Buffalo already had made known its intention of
leading off with O. J. Simpson, the Heisman Trophy winner
from Southern Cal. Among the other blue-chippers they considered were Purdue's Leroy Keyes, a two-way backfield star,
and George Kunz, Notre Dame's fine offensive tackle. Some
also included Hanratty in that company, but after what all
hands insist today was "brief" discussion, the Steelers dropped
him from first-round consideration.

They would go for Greene on the first round, if he was
available. The only prospects they were believed to rate above
him were Simpson and possibly Kunz.

Buffalo opened with Simpson and Atlanta followed by
choosing Kunz. Philadelphia opted for Keyes, who turned
out to be a flop, and then Pittsburgh chose Greene.

And then came Noll's complete vindication. Every other
team had picked in the first round and Hanratty was still un-
chosen. When the Steelers' turn came up again in the second
round, they went ahead and selected the Notre Dame quarterback. When they got to Hanratty, twenty-nine college
players had been chosen before him.

Noll's feelings about Hanratty have always been veiled, for
obvious reasons. Although Pittsburgh players feel Hanratty
has a better grasp of the offense than any other quarterback
who's been on the grounds in recent years, and they like him
immensely, Hanratty has never been given an open shot at the
starting job. Noll obviously has little confidence in Hanratty's

throwing arm, with reason. And, for all his talk about building a "supporting cast," the following year when a really outstanding quarterback did come along, the Steelers resisted a host of trades offering experienced bodies for the right to draft Terry Bradshaw. It all reminded some observers of Weeb Ewbank's comments about Hanratty. When the Jet coach was asked about the Notre Dame star, he diplomatically said he didn't want to take a chance on a quarterback with a bad knee. He hardly blushed when reminded that only four years earlier he had taken a first-round chance on a quarterback who was almost literally being wheeled into the operating room, Joe Namath.

Art Rooney, Jr., another of Rooney's sons, who serves as a Steeler vice-president and head of the personnel department, has his own theory about why Hanratty lasted into the second round. He said the club had Terry in for an examination of his knee the week before the draft. Other NFL teams knew this. Aware of how badly the Steelers needed a quarterback and how popular the drafting of a local kid out of Notre Dame would have been, they assumed Hanratty's knee was suspect if the Steelers passed him by.

Noll thus won both ends of his bet. Greene, who would not have been available in the second round, became a superstar. And, it turned out, nobody else in football thought Hanratty was worth a first-round choice, either. When it's suggested that Hanratty's availability in the second round doubly vindicated his judgment, Noll just smiles.

Greene's selection was greeted with less than indifference in Pittsburgh. Steeler fans get more emotionally involved with their team than supporters of any other NFL club this side of Green Bay. Years of failure had not dimmed this involvement, except perhaps to make it more cynical. Steeler fans expected to get dumped on. Their motto was S.O.S.: Same Old Steelers. They were shocked, but not necessarily surprised, when Pittsburgh picked an unknown defensive tackle from a mystery school as its number one draft choice. (By the same token, if the Steelers had gone for Hanratty, fan reaction would have been, "What's wrong with him?")

A Pittsburgh newspaper sent an inquiring reporter out into the streets to see if any local fans had ever heard of Joe Greene. There was not one positive response. The headline read: "Joe Who?"

The Steelers, of course, were chagrined. This was one of the most "professional" first-round picks they had made in years. They knew Joe Greene was a blue-chip football player, and so did everyone else in the NFL. Joe's agent was a fellow named Bucky Woy, who also handled golfer Lee Trevino. When Woy, for reasons of his own, passed these "Joe Who?" clippings on to his client, Greene was mortified. Pride is his most compelling emotion. He hadn't played a down and already Pittsburgh was demeaning him. He (and Woy) would make them pay.

Actually, Greene had been no more elated when the Steelers called his name than the man-in-the-Pittsburgh-street. The Steelers had a well-deserved reputation as losers, the town is not exactly one of America's garden spots, and Joe had been a Dallas Cowboy fan. On top of it all, he had expected to go one pick earlier, to Philadelphia, but Atlanta's choice of Kunz had upset his calculations. When he got the call from Noll saying he had been drafted by the Steelers, Joe said he was pleased but his soul came up empty. He thumbed through every sports book he could find, trying to find something good about Pittsburgh. He found nothing to console him. "It should have been a happy day, but it wasn't. It was a sad day, as if I hadn't been drafted at all," Joe recalls.

His spirits rose only a bit several hours later when he learned that a North Texas State teammate, defensive back Chuck Beatty, had also been tabbed by Pittsburgh, in the seventh round. At least he'd have someone to talk to in this alien land.

Contract negotiations between Greene and the Steelers started poorly, but this also has to be seen in the context of the times. This was the first year of the big rookie holdouts. O. J. Simpson and Leroy Keyes, among others, also were late in signing. O. J.'s connections started out asking for a $600,-000 contract.

"If O. J.'s asking for six hundred thousand dollars, maybe it will take a six-hundred-thousand-dollar man to stop him," Greene pointed out.

By July, Greene still had not signed, and Dan Rooney expressed his displeasure with uncharacteristic sharpness. "When Greene comes in here and shows us he's a football player, then I'll be willing to pay him what he says he's worth," Rooney snapped.

To which Joe replied, through the papers, "I'd rather play for ten dollars a game in the minor leagues than back down any further in the money I'm asking."

Because he did not have a contract, Greene declined to play in any of the preseason all-star games. But, on the day of the College All-Star game in Chicago, he and Dan Rooney came to terms.

No details were announced, but it is believed the three-year package, including bonus and incentive clauses, totaled nearly $200,000. Today Greene is probably in the $100,000-a-year class.

When he signed, Greene confessed that he almost wished he'd been drafted down in the second or third round, because "then I'd have been in camp from the beginning."

It is a credit to both sides that there was no residue of bitterness from the contract dispute, and the next day Dan Rooney drove his new employee to the Steelers' training camp at St. Vincent College in Latrobe, Pennsylvania, the town famous as the home of Arnold Palmer, Rolling Rock Beer, and the first pro football game ever played, in 1895.

Greene reported the night before the Steelers held their annual public intrasquad scrimmage in Latrobe. He would not participate in that exercise, so the next afternoon, while his teammates rested for their upcoming labors, Greene was sent off with an assistant coach and the trainer to be weighed and measured and timed in the forty-yard dash. Greene stands 6'4" and the scale stopped at 270 pounds. His striking features look as if they had been chipped from bronze. There are no round edges on his body, just corners and planes. Although he was never a weight lifter and thus did not have a weight lifter's sharply defined musculature, he exuded a massive strength. Today, with his beard, he looks like a biblical prophet.

It was a steaming hot day and line coach Walt Hackett and trainer Ralph Berlin doubted their watches when Joe Greene clicked off the forty-yard dash in 4.8 seconds. (By contrast, L. C. Greenwood, forty pounds lighter and known as a speed demon, runs a 4.7.) "I'd never seen a guy that big run that fast," said trainer Berlin, who admits he had half-expected to see an out-of-shape Greene fall out about the thirty-yard mark.

Joe Greene's pro career started in earnest the next Monday. Coaches call it an Oklahoma drill. That's the way it's described in the manuals. Another popular name is the "nutcracker," and it is one of the most brutal basic drills in all of football, designed for no other purpose than to measure a player's skill and love for contact. It is man on man, one step short of the gladiators' arena. Lips have been split, teeth lost, and knees disjointed in this drill. Careers have been ended in the Oklahoma pit as coaches on each side of the line goad their players to greater fury.

Basically, two blocking dummies are set up six feet apart to define the combat area. There is a ball carrier, an offensive lineman to block for him, and a defensive player to try to bring him down. The contest is between the blocker and tackler as, on the snap count, the ball is slapped into the runner's gut. Blood, sweat, dust, and fear—fear of being hurt, of being cut, of being humiliated—mix in equal amounts.

For a while Joe Greene stood and watched as one pair of Steelers after another grappled in the Oklahoma drill. Then, as the drill progressed, the players began to chant. "Hey, let's have number one. We want the number one." It was time for Joe Greene to prove himself. He had that gaudy number one tag and he had put himself on the line with his holdout. The first people he had to convince of his worth were his teammates.

Walt Hackett obliged. Joe Greene was sent into the pit against the blockers he would be facing in regular games, the guards. This was a comparatively strong position for the Steelers. Sam Davis and Bruce Van Dyke, starters then, are still in the NFL. The swing man was Ralph Wenzel, another veteran. One after another they took their stance, one after another they were sent dazed and sprawling into the dirt as Joe Greene slammed down the ball carrier. "He stretched out three of them on three successive plays, and after that nobody asked any more for the number one," recalls a man who was there.

From those moments on, even though the tempo and complications of pro football baffled him for a while because of his late start, Joe Greene was established as a pro in the eyes of his teammates.

"Joe from the beginning was like a child prodigy in music," recalls John Brown, a former Steeler who was an offensive tackle and team captain at the time. "He was the Cadillac of his class, like an André Watts on the piano. Sure, André Watts and Joe Greene both have to practice, but it's not the same as with the rest of us."

Brown, who became Joe's roommate and close friend, today is an executive with the Pittsburgh National Bank. He recalls the first time he ever faced Greene head-on in a pass protection drill. "I'd seen him running over those other guys and I was determined he wasn't going to run over me," says Brown, who had previously played for championship teams in Cleveland. "So instead of laying back waiting for him, I fired out to hit him first while he was still upright. Knocked him flat on his back and he looked up at me with this surprised expression on his face. It's the only time I ever caught him like that, though."

Once Greene became established, it no longer was necessary for him to prove himself in practice. In drills he concentrated on timing and techniques. But once in a while he would remind them of who he was.

Bob Fry, now an assistant with the Jets, was offensive line coach with the Steelers in Greene's early years. "One day during a pass protection drill, the guys were getting on Joe for something and he got a little angry," Fry recalls. "So he moved down the line and challenged every one of them, right in order. Left tackle, left guard, center, right guard, right tackle. Then the subs. He whipped about seven of them in a row, then he went off to the side and sat on his helmet."

Fry, who had played with Bob Lilly in Dallas, calls Greene "the best defensive tackle I've ever seen." He remembers that one of his major tasks each training season was to keep rookies from being discouraged in their workouts against Joe. Just because they couldn't handle number 75 didn't mean they couldn't make it in the NFL.

Once he got out into league warfare, Greene just as quickly made his presence felt, but he kept insisting that his reputation for mayhem was an embarrassment. So was his nickname, Mean Joe Greene. Greene stressed in interviews that the "Mean" appellation was guilt by association. His college team was known as the Mean Green, in honor of the school color. When he became the star, what better way to identify him but as Mean Joe Greene? It had such a nice ring. Eventually he'd learn to live with the nickname, which conjured up a caged beast slavering for raw meat, but to this day he still reminds interviewers, "My friends call me Joe. I like that."

The nickname, though, was permanently impressed on Greene during his rookie year when he was thrown out of a game for walloping Fran Tarkenton, then with the Giants,

long after that nifty quarterback had unloaded his pass.
Greene apologized for that one, sort of. "Sure I meant to hit
him. I just didn't realize it was so late. I sort of had a case
of tunnel vision," said Greene, who then added his regrets
that he hadn't "completed the job." Then he had to apologize
for those remarks, explaining he meant he wished he could
have completed playing the game. Sure.

Since this incident occurred in New York, home base for
most of the country's national media, Joe was branded from
then on as Mr. Mean.

On another occasion that year Joe was thrown out of a
game for a fight with the Vikings' Jim Vellone, who recalled
vividly the moment he turned around and his face "got well
acquainted with Joe Greene's fist." Joe said he was only pro-
tecting a teammate that time.

Later, Greene knocked out several teeth belonging to
Cleveland center Bob DeMarco, a former teammate, no less.
Press reports of the game relate that Joe "chased DeMarco
across the field," which is a bit of an unfair rap on Bob's
courage. As Green recalls it, the play was a screen pass and
DeMarco popped our hero once in the wrong place with an
elbow before he released to head off and form the screen.
Joe says he read the play and took off after DeMarco and the
play. Suddenly DeMarco stopped and turned. That was his
mistake. Greene, his adversary suddenly so close, dedentured
DeMarco with a forearm. After the season, Joe learned he
had been fined $500 by the league office for his aggressive
act, but that the Steelers had paid it for him.

The next year DeMarco is supposed to have talked about
plans for revenge, but if he hadn't really run away the first
time, on this occasion he did show some discretion. As they

lined up for the first play, DeMarco looked across the line of scrimmage and suggested, "Okay, Joe, how about a nice clean hard-fought game?"

When aroused, Greene is capable of superhuman feats, as in the victory over Oakland that put Pittsburgh into the Super Bowl when he ran right through the double team block of guard George Buehler and center Jim Otto and then flattened the running back who'd been kept in for extra blocking to sack quarterback Ken Stabler.

However, especially early in his career, there also were times when Greene's play, while always competent, was uninspired. It recalled some of those negative college reports.

That's why a couple of years ago a Viking scouting report is supposed to have included the following notation: "Don't make Joe Greene angry." Minnesota players were incredulous. They laughed. Out loud. But humorless Bud Grant as usual was not kidding. "I'm serious," he snapped, according to a player who was there. "Help him up after a play, pat him on the backside, talk to him. Keep him happy. If you get him angry, he's liable to hurt somebody."

Joe Greene always did inspire awe, even when he was a youngster growing up in Temple, Texas, about one hundred miles south of Dallas. Temple is noted for its proximity to Fort Hood and for its huge Veterans Administration hospital.

Joe actually was christened Charles Edward Greene, but those names, now attached separately to his two sons, were soon discarded. It was an aunt who began calling him Joe. His father was a carpenter and the Greenes had three more children before they separated. Joe was not yet ten years old when his father "just went somewhere." His mother worked from then on as a domestic to support the family, and Joe, as the oldest, would take care of the others after school.

Even today he takes a fatherly attitude toward his team-mates, especially the other members of the defensive line. It may have started from his experience as teenage man of the house. Even as a kid, he remembers, "I was the one my friends looked to for advice . . . and I started giving it."

Over the years he was always the biggest kid in his crowd. He was a serious kid, never seemed to laugh. His demeanor, coupled with his size, was forbidding, and he got an early self-described reputation for being "mean, a bully," even though he seldom got into fights.

The family moved quite a bit in those days, from one part of town to another, as Mrs. Greene struggled to make ends meet. She worked constantly, Joe remembers, but the kids were always neatly dressed, never felt deprived, and Joe has no memory of ever being on welfare. "We lived basically in a southern kind of ghetto. We weren't no different from any-body around us," he says.

He always worked and, as he grew older, he found himself side by side with grown men who had to support their fami-lies on little more than what he was making. That's when he vowed that somehow he wouldn't end up the same way. He figures that somehow he would have achieved the education to escape this trap, but in the end it wasn't necessary. Foot-ball provided the way. Embarrassed somewhat that he doesn't have his college degree, Joe Greene admits, "I sold out to football."

Football snared him by the time he was in the eighth grade. "Man, you gotta play football," the coaches crooned, and so he went out for the team. Later he would try baseball, but he couldn't judge flies and he was afraid of the ball.

There was too much running in basketball and he quit after one workout. He threw the shot and discus in track and eventually won a state championship.

But football was his game. He started for the jayvees as an eighth-grader and the next year moved up to the varsity as a first-string lineman. "I can't ever remember being second team," he says. From his sophomore year on he played middle linebacker for the Dunbar Panthers, an all-black school, even though as a senior he weighed 240 pounds. "I was probably the biggest middle linebacker in all of football," he laughs.

Football brought another advantage. Older kids once had liked to pick on him because he was as big as they were. But after he established himself in football, the bullies left him alone.

Even with Greene, Dunbar's record was mediocre, and the highest honor Joe ever won was all-district. Still, a couple of colleges were interested in furthering his football education. Texas A. & I. was interested, and so were New Mexico State and the University of Houston. Greene might have gone to Houston but that school called him down to visit the day of his senior prom. Joe decided to stay home and dance, and the Cougars, to their regret, took no for an answer.

One school Greene didn't hear from was North Texas State, and so he wrote to them. For some reason he was attracted to the school. Dunbar High didn't have the budget to film its games, but his coaches asked an opponent to send up movies of their games. North Texas saw the movies and invited Greene up for a visit, but Joe still thinks "they gave me a scholarship on my size."

That August, Joe Greene headed off for college, driven

there by his mother's employer. But those early days were depressing. It was hot, the drills were tiresome, and the campus was empty except for the football team, since classes had not yet begun. Joe Greene, away from home for the first time, almost quit. Fortunately, there was a break to go home at just the right time, and when he returned to campus, the student body was there and the place had come alive.

Joe played middle linebacker and guard as a freshman and started at guard and defensive tackle in his first spring practice. However, he lasted only a couple of days on offense. The temperament of an offensive lineman must be passive. Pass blockers absorb blows. Nobody able to carry the name of Mean Joe Greene—no matter how inappropriate he insists it is—can be an offensive lineman.

The North Texas freshman team was a good one, and it provided the nucleus for the Eagles' success the next three seasons. Once settled as a defensive tackle, Joe quickly moved up to the head of the class that spring and he started as a sophomore the following fall. That's when the Mean Green was born.

The year before, North Texas had been routed by Texas Western (now Texas–El Paso) by a humiliating 61–15 as Joe and his fellow freshmen watched from the stands. In the first game of Joe's first varsity season they met again, and this time North Texas came out on top, 12–9, holding the Miners to an incredible minus-forty-four yards rushing. (In college, quarterback sacks are counted against rushing yardage.)

Among those carried away by the victory was Sidney Sue Graham, wife of the North Texas sports information director. She thought her husband, Fred, should come up with a catchy title for this awesome defense. The school colors were green and white. "How about the Mean Green?" she asked brightly.

Fred Graham scoffed at the title as too corny, but the next week he inserted the name in one of his press releases. The name caught on, and today the school's teams are known no longer as the Eagles, but as the Mean Green. And when Joe Greene finished as an all-America and his number 75 became the first in school history to be retired, he had himself a nickname. During Joe's three seasons at North Texas, the school had a combined record of 23–5–1. The defense during that span allowed the opposition an average of less than two yards per running play. Joe was called by his coaches "a fort on foot." Despite an injured ankle that would require postseason surgery, one of Joe's best games came his junior year against Drake, when he blocked a field goal, forced a fumble, batted down a pass, and sacked the quarterback five times.

Joe Greene recalls his life at North Texas as placid and pleasant. Only four years earlier, integration had been less than popular at this state institution. Spider Lockhart, who graduated to a distinguished career as a safety with the New York Giants, recalls that when he went to NTS the football team had a quota of only three blacks and he was not encouraged to live on campus. When he and a teammate, tired of walking several miles each day just to get to class, did move into a dorm, students burned a cross on the lawn.

By the time Greene arrived, however, there were perhaps 2,000 blacks among the student body of 14,000, with seven or eight on the football team. "We were definitely in the minority, but we were treated well," Joe says. "We were the prize studs, I guess, but I didn't know any better then and I never felt unwanted."

The closest Greene came to exploding over a racial slur

was when some fraternity type insulted his wife, then pregnant with their first child. Greene charged over to the Kappa Alpha house prepared to wreak mayhem, but he was headed off by an apology. KA is known as an "old South" fraternity, and every once in a while Greene and the other blacks on the football team would charge their quarters and "run 'em all out of the frat house."

Lockhart became a major influence on Greene's life. After his first year with the Giants, Spider returned to the campus in the off-season to continue his studies. He adpoted the blacks on the football team, inviting them to his home for dinner, sponsoring excursions to Dallas or to a roadhouse just outside the town limits where the boys could have a beer. (Denton was dry.)

Lockhart had money in his pocket, dressed well, and drove a red Buick Riviera. (Joe still remembers the car.) More important, he had a polished and sophisticated air. Class. Joe Greene had never met a professional football player before, and Lockhart was a good one to start off with. Joe looked at Spider and said to himself, Hey, this is what I want. He set his mind to playing in the NFL.

Lockhart also remembers those days in Denton, Texas. Joe Greene was "a nice person, fun-loving; just like a baby, huge but nice." He wondered if Greene had the temperament to be a professional athlete; wondered, that is, until he saw Joe Greene in a game. "He's like a Jekyll and Hyde," Lockhart marveled.

When Greene later turned pro, Lockhart remembered the gentle giant with whom he'd once played dominoes. He couldn't believe it was the same guy leveling Fran Tarkenton in Yankee Stadium.

Also during this time at North Texas, Greene's life was

touched in a different way. He met a lovely, vivacious coed
from Dallas named Agnes Craft, and in his junior year they
were married. Agnes's background was decidedly different
from Joe's. Her father was a businessman, a member of the
black middle class in Dallas. Intelligent, level-headed, and
more outgoing than her shy husband, she kept Joe Greene's
cleats solidly attached to the turf as he moved into the heady
world of all-star teams, big money, and adulation.

The demands of superstardom keep Greene on the move
these days, even in the off-season, but Agnes, their three children, and the Greene home in suburban Dallas remain the
anchor of his existence.

When members of the Steeler family discuss their front
four, Dwight White emerges as the most stable of the group.
He arrived as a strong personality and player and he remains
so. Ernie Holmes is considered to have come the longest way
as a football player. L. C. Greenwood, who arrived as a rookie
hard-pressed to keep his weight as high as 220, has matured
the most physically.

But it is Joe Greene who has developed most as a personality and as a force on the team. Yet it took him virtually
until the Super Bowl season, his sixth as a professional, to
come to terms with his stardom. He still struggles with the
contradiction of his violent profession and an innate sensi-
tivity, but this is part of what makes him a fascinating individual, not a one-dimensional lump of mayhem and muscle.

Where are the roots of Joe Greene's complex personality?
Obviously back in Temple, Texas, where the oldest child
cared for his brothers and sisters, seeking eagerly for his
mother's approval.

"I was never the bully type," Joe Greene said one morning

over a huge breakfast—eggs, sausage, pancakes, milk, juice, and coffee—which he left half-finished. "My attitude, in fact, was not to offend anybody. I always said what I thought people wanted me to say and did what I thought they wanted me to do. I tried to 'buy' friends with kindness. I guess I still do."

And yet there also is a self-conciousness, a fear of looking foolish that sometimes reacts negatively to other people's embarrassment. Greene still finds it hard to accept that fans will utter inanities to him because they are flustered in his presence. He thinks they must be talking down to him.

"I don't want them to be in awe of me," he complains, "and I don't want to be your joke. Like, so many people who ask me about this Mean Joe thing really know how it got started. I get upset about that. I don't want to be nobody's entertainment. I'll do it for you on the field because that's my job, but I'll surely be glad when the autographs stop, no matter what they say about how you're supposed to miss it."

Greene's football philosophy is "I'm out there exhibiting myself, and what you see I want to look good." When an offensive lineman holds, it is an illegal way of keeping him from doing his job and thus making him look bad. This is what leads to many of his rages on the field. (Dwight White and Ernie Holmes are no different. Only L. C. Greenwood breaks the mold of defensive linemen and seems able to maintain his cool through all adversity.) Greene's temper has always been there and it explodes "if I think somebody is trying to make me look bad."

During Joe's first season with the Steelers, of course, there was little opportunity for him to exert leadership. He was a rookie, feeling his way, striving to maintain his pride with a team that lost more games in half a season than he had lost in his entire college career. When the final gun of the last game of the season sounded, Joe tossed the football into the stands in frustration.

Joe's second season he entered a different level of football and team politics. His wife came to Pittsburgh this time (Joe's weight soared to 280 on her cooking) and she and Mrs. Roy Jefferson became friendly. Jefferson was the Steelers' militant player representative and through their wives the two players became close friends.

This was the year of the first Players' Association strike, and feeling was high on both sides. Through Jefferson, Greene became heatedly involved in the strike and its issues. This was the first player strike in major league sports history and many members of the establishment reacted with shock. Pat Livingston, football columnist for the *Pittsburgh Press*, staunchly opposed the strike and day after day attacked the players and their aims. One day he and Jefferson ran into each other at a local golf tournament. They began debating the issues and Greene joined in. Frustrated in his arguments, he reacted by spitting in Livington's face.

Livingston did not write about the incident at first, but eventually it became public knowledge. Greene, when he realized what he had done, was abashed. But still proud. The Steelers called him in for a talk and eventually Joe apologized to Livingston, but with one condition: he did not want the apology made public. He did not want the fans to think he was crawling to curry favor with the press. He felt it was enough that Livingston realized man-to-man how badly he felt about the incident. Apparently Livingston agreed, and the two have since maintained a cordial relationship. If Pat had been vindictive, he could have ruined Greene's career in Pittsburgh. Livingston is a powerful and popular figure in that city, and very close to the Rooneys.

Even after the strike eventually ended, Jefferson remained an antiestablishment figure in the Steeler camp. He played his radio at top decibel in the dorm, parked his car in proscribed areas, was generally insubordinate, and demanded that his contract be renegotiated. Dan Rooney figured Jefferson just couldn't get used to the idea that the strike was over, like a combat veteran who can't adjust to peace.

The Steelers deny that Jefferson's close relationship to Greene had a direct bearing on what happened next, but within weeks the talented wide receiver, one of the team's few stars, was traded to Baltimore. More than one team has traded away a veteran because of his possible bad influence on a young potential star. But the Steelers insist that Jefferson was traded as a disruptive influence "on the whole team." Roy lasted only one season with the Colts, who traded him on to Washington, where he has lived happily ever after, and performed extraordinarily well.

As the year passed, Joe's outlook began to change. He bemoaned his loss of innocence and complained that football was "more fun in college." Moreover, as the Steelers began to improve, new tensions began to appear. Greene's sensitive antennae began to quiver as he picked up real and imagined vibrations from his teammates. No longer was he the single star of the defense. L. C. Greenwood had moved into the starting lineup, and White and Holmes had arrived.

The mother hen who had worried about his brothers and sisters and who wanted to be loved by all began to worry. How did his teammates react to all that Mean Joe Greene publicity? They had pride. Did they resent him? Did they resent his salary and his honors?

Over breakfast in Kansas City, where he had gone to receive an award, Joe Greene explained some of his inner turmoil:

"It began in 1971, when L. C. started playing and Dwight and Ernie came to camp for the first time. Dwight was always saying even then that he was playing in the shadow of Joe Greene, and I wondered how seriously he meant it. Ernie, when he started playing, immediately started thinking he could play as well as I could. L. C. felt he was as good as anybody in the league and he wanted to be paid for it.

"We had these personalities and I felt they thought I was taking something away from them with all the publicity I received. But it wasn't my fault and so I tried to make up for it in other ways. Hey, man, I just want to be with the group, too. I'm not trying to steal the show; I'm not distant from you. For a couple of years the battle went on. I'm trying to appease them with the little things I'm trying to do. Maybe they accepted me to a certain degree, but I think they were also trying to get into the position that I had gotten into in the NFL. Sometimes I felt they were holding it against me, that they felt the things I was getting were holding them back.

"The thing is we got past that this year, all the petty little stuff. I had always wanted Dwight to be Dwight and not chase me, but I also knew it had to be a helluva burden on these guys playing with a person like me. So I went overboard trying to rectify all that and then they'd say, 'Hey, man, what the hell you mean?' Like I wanted all of them to be all-pro and I'd pull as hard for them as I did for myself.

"I always felt guilty about going to the Pro Bowl, I really

did. I never could enjoy those things. Our team is a young team and we got a lot of good young players, but whether I deserved it or not, I've been in the Pro Bowl every year I've been in the league. In 1972, when we started winning, Franco or Shanklin made a statement that there were more people on the team than just a few stars, and that's when the city got behind every player. When we met Oakland in the play-offs, every guy on the team was represented by a banner in the stadium.

"But the season of 1973 was a bad year. We had bad times. I thought I had let the team down because I didn't hold up my end.* There would be talk after the workouts, a little cloud. It wasn't until then that I became aware of the thing about the sacks. Ever since I came to Pittsburgh we'd put up a little pot, a dollar or five dollars apiece to go to whoever got the most sacks in a game. I won most of the time, although L. C. was always close even when he didn't play all the time. But it created a little thing, and so we stopped it. I always like to get to the quarterback, but it wasn't a thing like I was trying to beat the guys on my team.

"The next year I did a lot of thinking about this, and what changed it was getting it out in the open. We stayed with it. We kept talking about being yourself, being your person. Don't worry about chasing me. You can't do what I do, but you all got your own way of doing things. Sometimes we started getting into that same old stuff again, but this time we talked it out right away.

"Look, we all have different personalities. I'm difficult at times. When it comes to playing football, I know as much

---

* Greene played most of the season with a bad back that made him fear for the end of his career.

about playing defensive end as I do about defensive tackle, and I tend to lean into other people's territory. Then it would be misinterpreted and we'd have squabbles about it. Instead of just worrying about myself, I tend to get nosey. But I call it being concerned. I want the whole thing to work right. Hell, all of 'em have been angry at me for something and I've been angry at them for something. As George Perles said to us once in a meeting, 'You know, coaching you guys ain't like handling just one bowl of cherries.'

"I'm the one most likely to give directions. Most of the time it's spontaneous. I don't think I'll do it if I know I'll hurt people's feelings, but I do it for the sake of the game. Our biggest arguments are about my talking, but the thing is I'd like everyone to get in on the communicating. Four heads are better than one. I never wanted the responsibility of being Joe Greene, the leader. I don't think I'm the leader type person. I just want to go out and do a good job and win. And I want the guys I play with to be on the same level.

"I got all that stuff off my chest this year. I had felt responsible for feeling guilty about making all-conference, but I don't any more. If you're going to trip on that trivia, go ahead. I used to be into it, too, because I was so busy fighting it, but now we've cleared those cobwebs. I was alone a lot this year because I didn't bring my family up to Pittsburgh with me and so I tried to do some thinking about myself. It was this thinking, I believe, that helped bring us together, the whole front four."

Greene says his outlook began to change at the close of the 1972 season when coach Chuck Noll announced in a squad meeting which players had been selected to play in the Pro Bowl. Greene and brainy linebacker Andy Russell, perennial choices, were selected again. Then Noll called out the names of the newcomers, Henry Davis, Roy Gerela, Franco Harris, and Dwight White.

"Everybody got a hand but Andy and myself," Greene recalls, the hurt still coming through in his quiet recital. "For what reason I don't know. Maybe it was supposed to be old hat for us. You talk about being low! That was the moment I felt for myself and for nobody else. It was my turn to be selfish and I took it that way. I felt I had given the guys everything I had to give, but that day I felt rained on, I sure as hell did."

After this hurt, it took Greene still another year of soul-searching, analysis, and give and take to establish working rapport with his three mates up front. But now it's there and, he says, "I couldn't stand to be around myself if I were the one to destroy it."

The irony, of course, is that so much of these supposed resentments and jealousies existed mainly in Joe's own mind. Certainly all of the other three at times had to resent playing in Joe's shadow and certainly all three sought to achieve stardom of their own. But resentment and jealousy of Joe's success? Dwight White articulates it best:

"All players, especially the type of players we have up front, are fierce competitors and nobody is ever happy to take a back seat. They want to be right on top and that's good from a competitive aspect. Joe was the superstar from the conception and there would be years other players would read the papers and it would be 'Joe Greene, Joe Greene,' and there didn't seem to be room for anyone else. But that didn't cause any real problems because that gave everyone incentive to reach for that number one spot. There was no animosity, just strong competition.

"Sure we all like to be applauded, but most of us have

reached the state of maturity to realize that feeling comfortable with yourself is a lot more important. The thing is, Joe is so sensitive, he's like a seismograph. Ever since I've known him he's been extremely perceptive and able to pick up just the smallest vibrations from people he's closest to. That's been good in some cases and bad in some cases, because that puts a bigger burden on him. He's so concerned about people that sometimes he overreacts."

Whatever the causes of the tension, whether it stemmed from his teammates' resentments or his own ultrasensitivity or both, Joe Greene was able to enter the 1974 season at the peak of his physical skills and able to accept the burden of leadership. Without sacrificing their own egos, whether it meant shaving their hair in the shape of an arrow or wearing gold shoes on the field, his teammates learned to live with it. And with themselves. And with each other.

3

Hollywood Bags

Coming down to the last week of the 1968 college football season, Art Rooney, Jr., was tired. He had been on the road all year, or so it seemed. His wife was sick. His kids were sick. It was gray December and why not cancel the last scouting swing that would take him through Arkansas A.M.&.N., as in Agriculture, Mechanical, and Normal. Today the school is known simply as the University of Arkansas in Pine Bluff.

Pine Bluff isn't exactly the beaten trail. It's forty-five miles southeast of Little Rock and one Steeler scout calls it "a quickie town, get in and get out."

Young Rooney, old Art's second son and a vice-president of the Steelers in charge of personnel, could have justified skipping this trip. Pittsburgh belonged to BLESTO, a scouting combine, with several other NFL teams, and the club already had a folder full of reports on A.M.&N.'s prospects. Still, the Steelers had been making a new commitment to the college draft as the way to reverse their losing program, and Artie had a guy he wanted to see in person: a wide receiver named Ed Cross. So Art Rooney, Jr., packed his overnight bag and his notebooks and headed off on one more trip.

Ed Cross looked all right. In fact, he was subsequently drafted by the Redskins on the third round that year. But Rooney's eye kept being drawn to a tall, lanky defensive end who was flitting through the agility drills like a ballet dancer and who ran like a halfback. The kid stood about 6'6" and weighed under 220 pounds. Rooney could hardly believe he played defensive end until he watched some film and saw that L. C. Greenwood had the knack of making the most spectacular plays. Terribly inconsistent, L. C. often got beaten, but those big plays stuck in Rooney's mind. Rooney left town before the weekend and never did see Greenwood play in a game.

Scouts look at players differently than anyone else, even differently than most people in football. After they finish weighing and timing and charting, they try to look through players with a sort of future vision to anticipate how they will develop. In seeking a scale for comparison, they often try to match the prospect against a known quantity. He reminds me of College Senior A, who is a known All-America and certain to go in the first round. Or he held his own against that same Senior A during a game. Sometimes the scout will figure, Pro Veteran B, who developed into a pretty good player, looked like that when he was in college.

Rooney's mental computer clicked away on the trip back from Pine Bluff. "Gee, this must have been what John Baker looked like when he was in college," the scout privately decided, recalling a defensive lineman who had rendered useful service to the Steelers a couple of years earlier. With that notation, Rooney filed away Greenwood's name for the upcoming pro football draft as a player who might be worth a shot in the later rounds.

Arkansas A.M.&N. had several players drafted that January, two of them by the Steelers. Greenwood's name was still on the board when the tenth round came up and the club followed Artie's hunch and grabbed him. "When you get to that point, you take people somebody has a feeling about," he explains. On the next cycle, they grabbed another defensive lineman from that school, Clarence Washington.

When Greenwood came in for spring rookie indoctrination, he was given two assignments. The first was a weight program to build him up, the second was to have his tonsils removed, which the club thought would make it easier for the pounds to stick. Eventually he built up to a program weight of 245, although late in any season he's barely within ten pounds of that figure.

As Greenwood developed first into a regular and then into a star, Art Rooney, Jr., began to feel pretty good about his draft choice, the tenth-rounder who made good. But then one day he ran into John Baker and he told the former Steeler how he had recommended drafting this Mississippi greyhound "because he reminded me of how you must have looked in college."

Baker, who had played at 270 pounds in the NFL, roared with laughter. "Well, you made a good pick, but for the wrong reasons," he shouted. "You see, when I was in college I weighed three hundred and ten pounds!"

It's the kind of story that keeps a scout humble.

When Greenwood and Clarence Washington reported to the St. Vincent College training base, they were hardly optimistic. Once the veterans arrived, they became downright pessimistic.

Washington was married and he missed his wife back home. Night after night he suggested, "Let's go home, man. We ain't gonna make it. All these guys are bigger, older, more experienced, and come from bigger schools. You can see what's happening. We're just here to make up the scrimmage lists."

But L. C. even then had learned to take the cool and reasoned approach, even though he was no more optimistic about their chances than Washington.

"Hey, man, there's no use in just going home," he would counsel. "We leave and we got to pay our own way. We should hang around till they send us. We ain't got nothin' to do now anyway. Let's wait till they cut us, then they got to pay our way home."

This fatalism may have helped these two rookies from a small black college. Fear—of making a mistake, of being cut—inhibits many a rookie. He goes out to every drill so tight it's as if his thighs were bound together in a vise. Thus hampered, he cannot freely show his skills, and eventually he is sent home. Pro teams avoid some of this by bringing the rookies in early alone so they can start out among their peers. But eventually the veterans report to cut the rooks down to size. The pressure of training camp is oppressive, especially for rookies, but there's pressure in games, too, and now is the time to find out who can handle it.

In any event, Greenwood and Washington unwittingly had figured out how to by-pass this fear of being cut. They just knew they were doomed and they clung together on and off the field for mutual comfort and protection. "We determined not to let ourselves get all broken up," Greenwood remembers. "Our object was just to protect ourselves until they gave us money to go home."

Too broke to go to town, they spent their free evenings sitting on the steps of the dorm watching the world go by.

Although convinced he wouldn't make it with the Steelers, Greenwood slowly began to realize that he was as good as most of the linemen in camp and better than a whole lot of them. He figured that when the ax did fall, he and Washington should be able to hook on with another team.

Even when the coaches praised him, Greenwood was suspicious of their motives. He played defensive end. Joe Greene, the touted number one draft choice who was holding out, also was talked of as a potential end. When good words about him appeared in the paper, L. C. figured it was just a political ploy to coax Greene into signing. But when Greene did appear, he was placed immediately at tackle, with no more mention of a switch to end. (Greene still has the speed to play end, but tackle is an easier position for a rookie to master. Because of Greene's late arrival, Steeler coaches may have decided to take the quickest route to getting their number one draft choice ready to pay off. They didn't want to waste time experimenting or teaching Greene a new and more complex position. It seems to have worked out for the best.)

Night after night, Greenwood and Washington expected to hear those fatal words: "Coach wants to see you, and bring your playbook." But the summons never came. Both, to their surprise, made the squad.

Actually, coaches at first thought Washington might be a better prospect than Greenwood, since he was built along more traditional lines for a defensive lineman. He was listed as 6'1", 214, not too big, but he appeared more stocky and figured to bulk out with age and a weight program. He also was further advanced in technique. However, after a year he hurt his knee and, once healed, never did advance beyond that initial plateau. In his third season he was cut. L. C., of course, blossomed.

It was during this first training camp that Greenwood earned the basic portion of his famous nickname. The late Walt Hackett was Pittsburgh's defensive line coach, and he had a tag line for everybody. For a while, L. C. was Greenbriar or Greenbush, but neither had a really catchy ring.

Then one day the coach hollered in L. C.'s direction, "Hey, Bags!" And that was it. From then on it was either Bags or Bag-It, and to this day nobody really knows why. Or will tell. Hackett died of a heart attack standing on the sidelines while scouting a college team at practice in the spring of 1971. This was before Greenwood became famous and nobody had ever bothered to ask him the inspiration for Bags.

The Hollywood part was added a year later. Greenwood early on had established his cool image and often boasted that he thought he could make it in the movies. The summer of 1970 there was talk that the Steelers were going to trade for a quarterback. Hottest rumor had Roman Gabriel of the Los Angeles Rams coming to Pittsburgh. The Steelers would give up Terry Hanratty and other players. Hanratty couldn't resist. He called Greenwood aside with a conspiratorial wink. "You're coming with me, I hear," he whispered. "We're off to the Rams and Hollywood. Get those bags packed."

Maybe L. C. didn't swallow the hook, but he sure nibbled at the bait. It's not known if he literally packed his bags, but he certainly was primed to go. Maybe some big Hollywood director really had suggested to the Rams that they "get this guy." Whatever, thanks to Hanratty's practical joke, he was now Hollywood Bags.

The name actually was the first that ever belonged to him, L. C. insists. The initials are just that. When he was born in Canton, Mississippi, all of the relatives wanted a piece of the action in naming Mr. and Mrs. Moses Greenwood's firstborn. Tired of all the haggling, Greenwood's dad decided to pin a pair of initials on the baby and that was that. L. C. it would be. Later eight more children would arrive and there would be plenty of names to go around without fear of offending any relatives. It was too late to do L. C. any good, however.

Moses Greenwood is now semiretired and runs a grocery store. When L. C. was a boy, his dad worked for the town as a custodian of sorts, and money was scarce. They lived in a little house and L. C. recalls Canton as "a great place to grow up." However, because times were hard, there was always work to be sought, and any money in his pocket was there because he had earned it.

Moses Greenwood would leave for work before dawn and during nonschool times he generally left behind a list of chores for L. C. The lists were long. "No way I could ever get all the work done, and when my daddy got home he'd ball me out for not finishing," L. C. remember without rancor.

However, there was one way to beat it. L. C. would get up even earlier in the morning and be gone before his dad awoke. He would then catch one of the trucks collecting workers to go out in the fields of the big farms and chop cotton. That way L. C. was out with his friends all day, he avoided the endless list of chores and the automatic chewing out from his father, and he'd get paid a few dollars. There was no pay for work around the house, of course, so even then, you might say, L. C. Greenwood was jumping leagues for better pay.

As he grew into his teens, L. C. determined to attend college. He wanted to be a pharmacist, and his dream was to own a drugstore. However, Canton's summer job opportunities for a young black were limited. Each vacation L. C. headed up north to stay with relatives in Chicago. He could get real jobs up there, for real money.

The cool image L. C. loves to project was probably born about this time. Chicago must have been a lonely place for this Mississippi small-town boy. He was surrounded by relatives, but they had their own lives to lead, their own jobs to hold. L. C. had to feel out of place when he was off working among street-wise Chicagoans. It would be necessary to adopt some veneer of indifference in this strange city. Later, returning with money in his jeans, what more effective pose for classmates who had remained home than the posture of the big-city swinger?

No doubt Hollywood Bags was born right there in Canton, Mississippi, and, as Dwight White puts it, "He's sold out; sold out to the way he is, and he's not going to change. He's created that image and that is it. It's not a fly-by-night thing that he's projecting, the way some guys change their thing every six months. His life is built around being Hollywood Bags; very cool, very together, and there's nothing wrong with that. He has some things he wants to do with himself and not only does he have direction but he also knows what he can't do."

Most of his teammates find Greenwood's pose amusing, but their laughter at the mention of his name is affectionate. They all know that inside Mr. Cool a shy and quiet introvert thirsts for recognition.

While articulate and well able to express himself, Greenwood is not long on conversation. His interview for this book, when transcribed, came out the shortest of the four. Some Steelers chuckle at the prospect of L. C.'s being paired in the same room with another celebrated Pittsburgh sphinx, Franco Harris. "They'd spend the whole year sitting on opposite sides of the room and you wouldn't hear a word out of either one," one chuckles.

"A hard kid to get close to," is the consensus in a Pittsburgh front office that prides itself on running a family operation.

L. C. didn't exactly burst into football. He played sandlot ball and the spring of his freshman year in high school went out for the team and apparently made the varsity. He was a running back.

However, when the coach called the players back to formal fall practice the next August, L. C. was sick in bed. It wasn't until two weeks later that he felt up to reporting, and by then the toughest part of the workouts were past. The coach thought this was no coincidence. "Doesn't look like you've got much charley," his word for heart or spirit, the coach said with a sneer. He gave L. C. his equipment but apparently did it in such a way that the youngster felt he didn't really want him around. "So I left."

For two years Greenwood played no formal football, but his senior year the school changed coaches and L. C. went out for the team again. He made it and played both ways in the line.

During this period, L. C. had concentrated on his studies and did well enough to qualify for academic scholarships at several schools. However, he also showed enough in that one year of high school ball to be offered some athletic grants as well. The athletic scholarships would cover more of his expenses—and that's how all-pro football players are born. Greenwood accepted a football grant at Arkansas A.M.&N., a predominantly black school nearly two hundred miles from home. The athletic program and facilities were not the greatest, even when compared to other black schools in the South, but it did have the courses he would need for pharmacy.

With this move L. C. pretty much broke his ties to Mississippi, although he still goes back to visit his folks, and after the Super Bowl, Canton celebrated L. C. Greenwood Day. How times do change! Today he makes his off-season home in Pittsburgh, where, even though he's a bachelor, he's bought a house. That's a typical move for the money-conscious football star. Why pay rent on an apartment when you can build equity in a home? What L. C. has never forgotten are the hard times, not the good times, pickin' cotton.

In college Greenwood was one of those combination defensive end-linebackers and personally he projected himself as a linebacker in the pros, once he got good enough to dream those dreams. His coach wasn't so easy to convince. Each year early in L. C.'s career a couple of big hulks out of high school or junior college would appear to challenge him for his job. "But those dudes all ended up by sitting on the bench," L. C. recalls with no little satisfaction.

Pharmacy was discarded early in Greenwood's college career. He says he just lost interest, but he did remain scholastically alive and he collected his degree in vocational education. He has taught in the off-season but doesn't like it. Business, or Hollywood, seems more his future. A big bonus that would help him establish some business, in fact, was what helped sway him toward signing with the World Football League.

When the Steelers sat down for the second day of the 1969 draft, Artie Rooney's voice wasn't the only one whispering L. C. Greenwood's name. Bill Nunn of the personnel staff also had seen him, and Nunn remembered the admonition of Chuck Noll, who had just been hired as head coach.

In essence, Noll had told the scouts, "Give me the good athletes. We can give them all the rest. We can build them up with weights, we can teach them techniques. But we can't make them athletes."

"L. C. epitomized what Noll had talked about," Nunn recalls. "He lacked techniques, he needed strength. But he could run like a deer. He was the kind of guy you had to bet on 'on the come.' "

"We drafted L. C. strictly on size and speed," says Noll. "In the remarks section of the scouting report he read like a very high draft choice, but in actual grades he was down the line. He turned out to be one of those lucky picks."

It was Greenwood's speed that attracted all eyes in training camp. He wasn't a tough guy and a lot of the veterans went to town on him. Mostly he worked against another rookie, Jon Kolb, a third-round draft choice from Oklahoma State, who seemed to be able to handle him easily. One coach remembers that L. C. occasionally was shifted to the other side, not only to build up his own confidence but so Kolb could get some better competition.

Indeed, there was discussion of cutting Greenwood that first season, but he still had that unreal speed and, as Noll remembers, "we were spotting L. C. and every time he got in there he got to the football. He kept catching our eye. We had to figure out a way to use him."

Despite his secret misgivings, Greenwood quickly fitted in. When Joe Greene showed up, he soon noticed "that jive dude from Mississippi who's already in with the veterans."

Greenwood also managed to avoid injury that critical first summer. He'll never be known as one of the great Spartans. When he hurts, everybody knows it. However, as Joe Greene puts it, "L. C. hasn't been healthy since that first summer—but he always shows on Sunday."

Actually, the seeds of L. C.'s future flirtation with the WFL were planted in 1969. As a low-round draft choice from a small black school with little leverage, L. C. received a low base salary. He got perhaps a $5,000 signing bonus, but his salary on three one-year contracts signed all at once was probably under $20,000. Then, because he failed to make a quick move to establish himself as a regular, much less as a star, it remained comparatively low for several years. It probably wasn't until after the 1972 season, his second as a regular and the Steelers' first in the playoffs, that L. C. could demand a really good raise. Even so, he was probably making a third or so of Greene's salary.

"You start low and it's a helluva long road up there," Greenwood explains. "It really gets discouraging, too, when you know you're doing as well or better than the other guys who are up there and you know the guy beside you is making three or four times as much."

Greene typically is not insensitive to this situation. He feels black players, especially those from the small black schools, are exploited in the NFL. It's not so much venality on the part of club owners but because these players do not have the sophisticated representation of their white counterparts. Often they are not as sophisticated themselves, either, which leads to dual exploitation, as Ernie Holmes would learn the hard way. Greene feels perhaps the Players Association should play a role in this area.

Greenwood was discussing his future several weeks after the Super Bowl. He had not yet officially become a free agent, since his contract did not expire until May 1. He did not know if he would be going to the WFL or to another NFL team or back to the Steelers. We talked in the conference room of the Steelers' office complex beneath Three Rivers Stadium. Because of the ambiguous contract situation, many players might have felt uncomfortable in these surroundings. Greenwood did not. The Steelers would not allow it.

When L. C. reported to training camp, his 1976 WFL contract freshly signed, Dan Rooney called L. C. aside. "Look, we want you to feel at ease. As far as we're concerned, you're still a Steeler," Rooney told him. On this day, months later, L. C. was greeted with smiles and handshakes and a yelp of surprise—"Bag-It!"—from the man he responded to as "Witch Doctor!"—trainer Ralph Berlin.

Pride, as much as anything, had propelled L. C. to listen to the WFL offers, even though he admitted just before the Super Bowl that he was sorry about getting mixed up with what had developed into a financially unstable enterprise.

(Birmingham had won the WFL championship, yet at the end of the season their uniforms were repossessed and there were tax liens against the franchise. "But if the money's right, I'll bring my own shirt next year," L. C. joked.)

"To me it was as if they were dissatisfied with my performance," Greenwood said of his negotiations with the Steelers. "If I'm doing as well as anybody else on the team or as other guys in the league, I should get as much."

The WFL had picked a good time to make its initial approach to Greenwood. It was after the 1973 season and he had just been chosen for the first time to play in the Pro Bowl. The game was scheduled for Kansas City, but practice had been shifted to San Diego because of a Midwest blizzard. Greenwood's contract had an option year to go and he had just been officially anointed as one of the NFL's best. WFL headquarters were being established in Anaheim, California. Their people cornered L. C. and others in nearby San Diego.

At first, he says, he did nothing to encourage the new league's agents, but they persisted. Finally, what the hell, he went down to Birmingham to hear them out. Their proposal was well beyond anything the Steelers had offered, notably a $250,000 bonus with $40,000 payable up front, which he indicates he has received.

When they heard these figures, even the Pittsburgh people said he owed it to himself to take the money and run for Birmingham.

Pragmatic Art Rooney, Sr., owner of the Steelers, had only one word of advice for Greenwood as they discussed his impending decision to jump at length for the first and only time.

"If you're getting that kind of price," Rooney said, refer-

ring to the Birmingham boodle, "make sure that you're getting it, that they've got the money in the bank and that it's
yours. That's the only advice I can give you, because I don't
know how they can afford these things. I know what we get
for TV and we're sold out at home and sold out just about
every place we play, and if we can't afford it, I don't know
how they can afford it."

Rooney said he never had any concern that Greenwood
would dog it during his lame-duck season, and it turned out
that L. C. enjoyed his best and most spectacular year.

Although Steeler brass knew Greenwood was going to
jump, most of them had to read about the actual event in the
newspapers. Visiting back in Texas, Dwight White heard
the news on the radio and for once he had no speech to de-
liver. Oops, he thought at the prospect that the front four's
delicate balance might be disrupted, and that said it all.

Soon afterward Bill Nunn ran into Greenwood on the
street in Pittsburgh. "Look, I'm really a little upset with
you," Nunn said in mock severity, but only half kidding. "I
really wanted that [Super Bowl] ring."

He was half-asking whether Greenwood intended to go all
out or whether he would play it safe and protect his body
for the big WFL payoff.

"Look," Greenwood answered with uncharacteristic seri-
ousness. "If I make the move, this is going to be my last shot,
too. You better believe I'm going to play my ass off this
year."

Nunn wouldn't have been concerned if he'd been listening
in to a phone conversation the day Greenwood signed with
the WFL. The only known call L. C. made to any member of
the Steeler organization to announce his signing was not to

any coach or manager or owner, but to the leader of the defensive line, Joe Greene.

"Well, I signed with the World Football League," Greenwood said. "I didn't want to do it, but that's the way it went down."

Then he added the clincher as he referred to himself and his three colleagues on the front four and what they had been striving for: "This is the last time we got to do it. We got to do it this year."

4

Same Old Steelers

Mean Joe Greene and his mates really enjoyed the moment as they trotted out onto Tulane Stadium's Poly-Turf to play for the world's championship of professional football. They had come such a long way they didn't feel the need to sympathize with any of their rivals on the twenty-four NFL stay-at-home teams who would be watching on television. The Steelers had paid their dues.

"The worst team in pro football has it easy compared with my first year in Pittsburgh. I don't think football can get any worse," Joe Greene had said earlier during Super Bowl Week.

"I don't think we could have started out any lower than we did, except maybe to go 0-and-fourteen. As it was, we were one-and-thirteen, but I think we really had an 0-and-fourteen team."

Actually, the Steelers came within minutes of being winless in Greene's rookie season. Warren Bankston, a rookie running back whose fumble had just set up Detroit's go-ahead touchdown, ran six yards for the winning score with three minutes left for a 16–13 victory over Detroit in the season opener.

The rookies were impressed. Boy, we got a heckuva team, L. C. Greenwood remembers thinking.

From then on it was downhill to disaster. The Steelers lost every one of their remaining games. Thirteen in a row.

A brief catalogue of some of those defeats tells more than anything else what kind of season it was.

In game two, 41–27 to Philadelphia as Norm Snead throws five touchdown passes; 27–14 to St. Louis as three interceptions and a fumble give the Cardinals twenty points in the second period; 10–7 to New York as the Giants are able to move into range for what proves to be a winning field goal after Joe Greene is ejected; 42–31 to Cleveland, Steelers scoring twenty-one points in the fourth quarter, but the Browns do, too; 14–7 to Washington, blowing a 7–0 lead on two Sonny Jurgensen touchdown passes in the third quarter; 38–34 to Green Bay as injured Bart Starr comes off the bench to throw the winning touchdown pass with five minutes left; 52–14 to Minnesota on four interceptions; 47–10 to St. Louis, giving up twenty-eight points in the last quarter; 21–17 to New York as Tarkenton throws his third touchdown pass for a winner with forty-eight seconds left; 27–24 to New Orleans on a touchdown run by Andy Livingston with fifty-six seconds left.

(There would be some irony involved in that closing defeat by the Saints, coming as it did in the same New Orleans stadium where five years later the Steelers would climax their greatest season.)

There was little satisfaction for the Steelers in all the close games they played. Bad teams lose games in the last quarter and the Steelers proved it. Despite an outstanding rookie season by Greene, the defense was terrible. Pittsburgh was the only team in the NFL to surrender more than four hundred points.

Once the Steelers' skid began, Greenwood and the others became reluctant to tell fans they were football players. The admission would trigger a stream of abuse. They'd ask L. C. what position he played. "Defensive end? No wonder the Steelers lose so many games. They got ol' skinny guys like you playing defensive end."

During times like these, Greenwood was glad he didn't look like a football player.

Greene, however, had no such cover. He was an instant celebrity in Pittsburgh, the "Joe Who?" days long forgotten.

Noll admits that one of his most important coaching jobs that season was to see that Joe Greene, his foundation for the future, did not get discouraged and fall back into the morass of defeat and despair that had already drowned some of the team's veteran talents.

Greene recalls that first professional season as composed of almost complete misery despite his instant stardom, season-long accolades, and postseason awards. He lived in a downtown hotel with Chuck Beatty, his classmate from North Texas State, while Agnes and the boys remained in Dallas. He was lonely and depressed and he missed his family and familiar surroundings. Pittsburgh can be a dreary place for a stranger under the best of circumstances. For a lonesome young black from Texas it was almost unbearable, especially since the team was constantly losing.

"It seems like we played for months and months, but I don't remember November at all," Joe says today.

At least there was little dissension or bickering on the

team. Only ball clubs that have once known success have
dissension.

"The guys were just too comfortable in losing to bicker
among themselves," Greene says. "Every Sunday they'd go
out and wonder, Well, what's going to happen to us this
time? We were drowning in that 'Same Old Steelers' stuff."

The next year in a preseason game, Greene remembers
being incensed when he went out on the field to face the
Miami Dolphins as one of the veterans, anticipating defeat,
yelled out, "Well, let's try to keep it close."

Conditions for the Steelers that first year were dismal.
Three Rivers Stadium, with its plush offices, dressing rooms,
and training facilities, was still under construction. It would
not be available for another year. The Steelers played their
games at Pitt Stadium, home of the University of Pittsburgh,
but they were like transient boarders who showed up only
on Sundays. During the week they worked out at South
Park, a fairground on the other side of town that came to
life for a few days around Labor Day once a year. The rest
of the time it idled and rotted. The team dressed in the
basement of the first-aid building. During bad weather they
practiced in a dusty barn. Toilet and shower facilities were
primitive.

As the losses mounted, Greene became a frequent visitor
to Dan Rooney's office in downtown Pittsburgh. He was
seeking reassurance. Would his whole football career be
spent in this losing situation? He had questions to ask. When
are we going to start winning? What's the front office doing
to turn the program around? Is there anything I can do?

Rooney tried his best to keep Greene's spirits up. As for

what the big rookie could do, "You could take over more of the role of team leader," Dan suggested.

"Aw, I'm no leader, I'm a football player," Greene would mumble in reply.

Still, despite his reluctance to assume the role, the seeds of responsibility were being planted. He spent time visiting the coaches, too. "We're losing. What more can I do to stop it?" he would ask.

In a sense, Chuck Noll was going through the same kind of rookie trauma, since this was his first season as a head coach on any level of ball.

Greene says he can remember occasionally catching Noll in an off-guard moment on the practice field with what the big tackle calls a "Why me, Lord?" expression on his face. "Chuck didn't swear much when he first came to Pittsburgh, but each year he seems to have added a few words to his vocabulary," Greene says.

Noll had been reared on success in such places as Cleveland, San Diego, and Baltimore. Although the losses mounted, players and management became increasingly impressed with the phlegmatic Ohioan.

"He never lost the team," marveled owner Art Rooney, and veterans recalled years later how Noll never gave up on them or on his program, or allowed the players to give up on themselves.

"He never panicked," a survivor said. "He convinced us that we were making progress, and if we stuck with him and his program, eventually would be winners."

The hiring of Noll marked a critical turn-around for the Steelers, who for many years had operated on an almost informal family basis. Pro football in Pittsburgh was literally fun and games. The losing grated on Art Rooney's soul, but he continued to hire his friends as coaches and then he allowed them to run the team with a free hand. "Maybe," he admitted later, "I should have interfered more."

Finally, in the 1960s, mobilized first by an all-out challenge from the American Football League and then by the prospect of even greater profits (and competition) when the two leagues merged, the Steelers got themselves organized. They continued as a family-run enterprise, but on a business-like basis. Dan Rooney was placed in charge of the front office, Art Rooney, Jr., in charge of a new professionalized scouting program that would include both the colleges and the pros. The Steelers became their full-time job. The club would be moving into a brand-new stadium soon. There would be a $3 million bonus for agreeing to move (with Baltimore and Cleveland) into a new conference with their former rivals from the AFL. Television revenue was increasing and the expensive war for talent had ended. Money was pouring in. The Steelers would have no excuse not to become competitive.

Hard-drinking Buddy Parker had been coach for eight years, but he quit abruptly before the 1965 season when Dan Rooney for the first time challenged his authority. Mike Nixon filled in for a year with 2–12 results and then, for the first time, the Steelers went outside their circle of "old boys" to name Bill Austin as head coach. Austin, a former Giant player who had coached under Vince Lombardi in Green Bay, was a mistake. Over three seasons his losing records grew progressively worse. Austin was released after going 2–11–1 in 1968, and the search for a new coach began.

The Rooneys' first choice for this job was Joe Paterno,

highly successful coach at Penn State University, 125 miles east of Pittsburgh. Paterno, one of the nation's leading young coaches, had grown close to the Rooneys since coming to Penn State as an assistant in 1950. In three years as head coach, he had compiled a 24–7–1 record. That past season the Nittany Lions had gone undefeated and had beaten Kansas in the Orange Bowl, and Paterno had been named "Coach of the Year." Paterno is a native New Yorker, which may have abetted the empathy with Art Rooney, Sr. Both are "street smart." With Paterno, already famed as one of the new breed of college coach who liked to have his players graduate, the Rooneys felt they could make a long-term commitment. And get one in return.

As a matter of fact, the deal was sealed at one point. For a huge sum, reported to run over $1 million, and a long-term contract, Paterno agreed to take over the Steelers. Paterno then went home to tell his wife. According to friends, she broke into tears. Suzanne Paterno is from Latrobe, Pennsylvania, and attended Penn State, where she and Joe met. Home for the Paterno clan (four children at that point) was State College, Pennsylvania. It was a delightful place to bring up kids and, in that environment, Paterno's salary, with various emoluments and perquisites from grateful alumni and boosters, was more than adequate. In a few years, Paterno, as a tenured faculty member, would be eligible for a large pension.

Joe Paterno, then as now completely dedicated to his family, had to call back and respectfully decline the offer.

Stymied in this direction, the Steelers turned back into the professional ranks. In this kind of building situation, there are two alternatives. One is to hire a veteran coach who has been through many campaigns. He will be patient. He knows that no matter how dismal the Sunday afternoon, a new sun usually will rise the next morning. (Although in the old days before Pittsburgh licked its smog problem one really couldn't be sure.)

The other alternative is to choose a completely dedicated young man who, as Casey Stengel liked to put it, "has never failed."

The Steelers came down to one from each school: forty-seven-year-old Nick Skorich, a former Steeler player and now an assistant with the Browns after three years as head coach of the Eagles; and thirty-seven-year-old Chuck Noll, an assistant coach with the NFL-champion Colts.

Perhaps Skorich, who later became head coach of the Browns, was too close to the old Steeler family. The Rooneys hired Noll.

Old Art Rooney, a racing guy all his life, figured Noll had to be a success. "He's by Don Shula out of Sid Gillman by Paul Brown," Rooney said, using breeding terminology to refer to the three great pro coaches with whom Noll had been associated.

In racing there's another saying: "You breed the best with the best and hope for the best," and that's how it worked out for the Steelers. Noll turned out to be a perfect choice.

In many respects, Noll was a self-made pro player. Although he'd made all-state for Benedictine High of Cleveland as a two-way guard, bigtime colleges did not seek his services. He ended up at the University of Dayton, where he played tackle on offense and linebacker on defense, plus some defensive back. He did get noticed in the draft, but only barely. His hometown Browns picked him in the twentieth round after some two hundred players already had been selected and offered him a $5,000 contract. He signed.

Noll weighed only 215 pounds, but he was quick and he was smart. Both attributes helped him succeed in Cleveland. Paul Brown called all the plays for his quarterbacks and he alternated two guards to send his orders into the huddle. To do this he needed two guards who were fast enough to get on and off the field in time and smart enough to remember the plays. They also, of course, had to be able to play, and so for seven years Noll was a messenger guard and then a linebacker for the Browns. During this period they won four division championships and two NFL titles.

During the final years of his professional career, Noll unveiled one of the character traits that would help him so much when he became a coach. He knew he would not be playing indefinitely, and so he methodically began to explore other possible vocations. He tried law school one off-season, he represented a trucking line, he sold insurance. He found himself drawn to none of them. Only in football did he find complete satisfaction, and now the final alternative was clear in his mind. He would be a coach.

Noll was still an effective player and earning $9,700 a year when he decided to make his break. (The fact that he still had some good years left may be the source of the cold feeling between Noll and his old mentor, Paul Brown, which exists to this day.) There was an opening on the staff at Dayton and Noll applied for the assistant's job at his alma mater.

However, although turned down for the job at the last minute, with Teutonic singleness of purpose befitting his German ancestry, Noll refused to waver from his commitment to quit football as a player. The American Football League was just cranking up for its inaugural season of 1960, and Sid Gillman, former coach at Miami of Ohio and the NFL Los Angeles Rams, was putting together a staff for one of the new teams. At twenty-seven, Noll became a defensive coach with the Los Angeles Chargers. After one year the team moved to San Diego and Noll remained with them through 1965. In six years the Chargers won three championships.

In 1966 Noll returned to the NFL as defensive backfield coach with the Baltimore Colts. In 1968 the Colts made it into the Super Bowl, and that championship performance provided the springboard to Pittsburgh.

As you look back at Noll's career, it's easy to see his need to control the events in his life. Moves are carefully charted, alternatives considered. When Chuck Noll says, "Good morning," he seems to have thought about it.

"The man wants to do everything. He's got to be in control, he's got to have that power," a former player analyzes. "The thing is he's a really bright football man and he can do it."

Noll gives the impression of complete self-control as well, and this is the attitude he expects from his players. Many of them feel he would really prefer to be coaching the Miami Dolphins, a team of ultraprofessionals who enjoy no peaks and suffer no valleys and who often act as if they should be carrying attaché cases out on the field.

"Chuck Noll is a very unemotional and calculating coach, and he would like his team to be like that," his former player adds.

Noll's approach does create a split in the Steelers' team personality. The players, generally, are an emotional bunch, almost collegiate in their ups and downs. That's their style. Even outsiders could exult with them as they openly enjoyed their Super Bowl success. Those close to the team speculate that it is owner Art Rooney who bridges this emotion gap. His paternalism—and this is paternalism among equals—provides the team with its dominant character and much of its warmth.

Noll denies the accusation—or description—of unemotionalism.

"Football is emotional," he says flatly. "It's not a normal thing to run down the field and run into somebody. You have to convince yourself that that's the thing to do."

Noll stressed that he was talking from his own experience as a player. "Nobody can be involved in this game and be emotionless, because emotions are involved," he continued. "People on TV or in the movies can portray emotion, but just because you don't portray emotion doesn't mean it's not there. I can be sitting here and have emotion welled up inside me, but you're not going to be able to tell."

What Noll overlooked, however, was that many players relish the contact of football and do not have to convince themselves that hitting people "is the thing to do." One man's emotion can be another man's cool calculation.

Long-time members of the Steeler family confess that sometimes they feel uncomfortable around Noll, even in social situations. Talking to him, one gets the feeling of being constantly tested. Even Joe Greene, who likes him, calls Noll "a hard man to talk to."

As a man who has played both offense and defense, Noll has the background to oversee the entire game plan and he has the intelligence and concentration to manage it. But his determination to be in control also is reflected in a fairly heavy turnover in assistants.

Noll, married and the father of a teenage son, is perhaps one of the most complex and interesting coaches in the NFL. Many of his colleagues care little beyond their Xs and Os. They reached their positions—and remember, this exclusive clan numbers less than thirty—by complete dedication to the single pursuit of football victory.

Noll is no less dedicated, but his sweeping intelligence allows room for other esoteric interests. He is a gourmet, a connoisseur of fine wines, a lover of classical music, especially from the baroque period. He likes scuba diving and, after the Super Bowl victory, took flying lessons. He is probably the closest thing to a renaissance man in professional football coaching. He might be the most interesting coach of all to know, if he'd drop his guard and allow it.

Noll works well with the press and possesses an intelligent sense of humor. He often uses one to keep the other at bay, and has been known to turn away questions he prefers not to answer with a cutting humorous retort. Often the victim doesn't even realize he has been skewered. "He uses his sense of humor to maintain control of situations," his former player says.

When the Steelers went to the Super Bowl, Noll not only encouraged the players' wives to come down a few days before the game, he committed Spartan heresy by allowing them to move right in with their husbands. Some of the older coaches like to joke about their "Tuesday rule" under which they "tell the married players to stay away from their wives after Tuesday and tell the single guys we hope they don't get lucky." However, Noll may have remembered his losing

Super Bowl experience with the Colts when the Jets had allowed wives and children to come down with the team ten days before the game. Most of the pro football establishment thought this foolish, but the Jets, preparing for the game family style, won easily.

When asked about this early in the week, Noll responded seriously, "We don't consider the wives a distraction. Most of our players chose them a long time ago and we consider them a plus."

Later in the week the question was repeated by newsmen recently arrived on the scene. Why let the wives move in so close to game time? This time Noll responded with a story.

Several years before, when the Steelers were struggling, they had been approached by a dietician who suggested a new type of pregame meal. Instead of steak and potatoes, he proposed a concoction of all the right vitamins and minerals mashed up in a blender and taken through straws like a milkshake. Dietetically speaking, his theory was sound, and, as Noll recalled the moment, "at that time we were willing to try anything." One Sunday the Steelers tried their new pregame glop—you couldn't call it a meal—and in graphic terms Noll described the epidemic of diarrhea, cramps, and flatulence that spread up and down the sidelines during the afternoon.

Some writers laughed uproariously at the story, others looked blank. "What's that got to do with having the wives in?" one of the mystified majority finally asked.

"I'm afraid you'll have to do some parallel thinking to figure that one out," Noll replied dryly, and passed on to other matters.

A sense of humor can be just as valuable when you're

1-and-13 as when you're going for the Super Bowl, but single-ness of purpose is important, too.

The Steelers' determination to follow their rebuilding game plan was put to the test after Noll's first season.

In his initial draft he had obtained such blue-chippers as Greene, Hanratty, and tackle Jon Kolb, plus two other rookies who would produce in the future, Greenwood and free agent offensive lineman Jim Clack.

That 1–13 record gave Pittsburgh lead-off position for the 1970 draft after Dan Rooney won a coin flip with similarly hapless Chicago, and this year the spot was considered invaluable. There was a senior quarterback down at little Louisiana Tech named Terry Bradshaw, considered by most scouts the best thing to come along since sliced bread and Joe Namath. And, unlike Namath, he was physically sound. Bradshaw, also dangerous running the ball, was a scouting computer's dream: 6'3", 215 pounds, and with a rifle instead of a mere mortal arm.

In the weeks before the draft, team after team besieged the Steelers with trade offers for that lead-off spot. Jet coach Charley Winner, then with the St. Louis Cardinals, says he offered Pittsburgh "five potential regulars plus our own first-round choice" for the shot at Bradshaw. Another team offered as much. (Noll today says the offer consisted of "second-liners.")

The Steelers, however, had made their determination early. They would listen out of courtesy—and maybe somebody would come up with an offer they couldn't refuse—but they would not budge. Once, back in 1939, they had traded away their number one draft choice and the Chicago Bears had converted that pick into Sid Luckman. Johnny Unitas had been a Steeler, only to be discarded in his first training camp as "too dumb." (Maybe the Steelers were right. Two of the guys they kept were Jim Finks, now general manager of the Chicago Bears, and Ted Marchibroda, head coach of the Baltimore Colts. They probably were smarter than Unitas— only he could play quarterback.) Len Dawson, Jack Kemp, Earl Morrall, and Bill Nelsen, all of whom appeared in championship games before the Steelers got there, had been discarded. "Yep," laughs Art Rooney, "we sure know a lot about quarterbacks."

The Steelers decided they would not risk this kind of embarrassment again. As they put it now, refusing offers for the rights to Bradshaw became "a management decision."

Noll obviously agreed. For all of his "supporting cast" talk the year before, he knew that when you've got a shot at one of those superquarterback prospects, you grab him.

Although he came from a little-known college, there was no sense of a Terry Who? when the Steelers drafted Bradshaw. Although he attended a supposedly small-time college division school, he had made several major all-America teams and was named Most Valuable Player in the prestigious Senior Bowl.

The Steelers followed up by tabbing Ron Shanklin, a wide receiver from Joe Greene's alma mater, North Texas State, in the second round, and on round three they picked Mel Blount, a cornerback from Southern University. All three would survive to start in the Super Bowl.

Greene pronounced himself as "overwhelmed" by the draft.

Not long after, he talked about these decisions and what they meant to him as a young player sure of his own talents but still questioning the surroundings in which they'd be displayed. The draft assured him that the Steelers weren't going to stick with over-the-hill losers who worried not about winning but with just keeping scores close.

"Coach Noll and Dan Rooney had a plan to bring the Steelers out of the dark ages, and the courage to stick with that plan. They decided to go for youth, for high-quality athletes with little experience, and then wait for them to mature. Those guys had plenty of time to panic, but they stuck with their commitment," Joe declared.

One day during his second season, Greene began counting names on the Steeler roster. Only seventeen of forty men were still around from his rookie year. Only ten of this number—just five of them from the pre-Noll era—would make it to the Super Bowl.

Center Ray Mansfield, who had arrived in 1964 in a trade from the Eagles, was one of the before-Noll veterans. "You know," he reminisced one day, "I used to think those guys playing beside me in those days were pretty good ball players. I couldn't understand why we kept losing."

Linebacker Andy Russell, who had been a sixteenth-round draft choice in 1963, had an answer. "Maybe that was because we weren't any better than they were."

But to Greene, who could be a little more detached than the older veterans whose friends were being cut, the players Noll had eliminated were mostly deadwood.

5

Mad Dog

Not all the players shipped out by Noll before his second season could be classified as deadwood. In a major shocker at the beginning of training camp in August of 1970 he suddenly dispatched Roy Jefferson to the Baltimore Colts in exchange for another experienced receiver, Willie Richardson, and a fourth-round draft choice.

This move took courage because Jefferson was one of the team's few established stars, an all-pro. However, he had become such a disruptive influence that a deal had to be made. It was a case, to use baseball manager Gene Mauch's expression, of "addition by subtraction."

About the same time, Noll decided it was foolish to carry two veteran centers when only one would do most of the playing. He cast his vote for Ray Mansfield, who would have his best season at age thirty-three as Pittsburgh won the Super Bowl. Bob DeMarco was traded to Miami for a mere eighth-round draft choice. (DeMarco later would end up in Cleveland as a future Joe Greene sparring partner.)

Also during this house-cleaning, Ray May, well regarded

by many as a linebacker, was traded to Baltimore for a package that included running back Preston Pearson. When the Steelers finally made it to the Super Bowl, Noll and Pearson, who had become a useful back, were the only ones on the squad who knew what it was going to be like.

The Jefferson deal, naturally, created the most stir in Pittsburgh. Flamboyant, outspoken, and highly skilled, he was the most visible of all the players Noll sent away, and he provided further embarrassment by catching forty-four passes for the Colts to finish seventh in the American Conference while not one Steeler rated in the top twenty. Then, to put himself further on the spot, Noll quickly deduced that Willie Richardson at age thirty was finished as a ball player. Within a month, Richardson also was sent south to Miami for a fifth-round draft choice.

So, as the Steelers and their rookie quarterback, Terry Bradshaw, struggled through a 5–9 season, they really had nothing to show for Jefferson, or DeMarco, either. It would be months before the college draft when they at least had names to fill in for those vacant slots and months more before they found out whether the new bodies would produce.

As important as the selections of Greene and Bradshaw had been in the previous two years, the heart of Pittsburgh's Super Bowl team came from that 1971 draft. It may have been one of the most productive in pro history.

With their first four picks, the Steelers chose wide receiver Frank Lewis, linebacker Jack Ham, running back Steve Davis, and offensive lineman Gerry Mullins, all of whom would play critical roles in that championship season.

Then, with their second fourth-round choice, obtained

from Baltimore for Roy Jefferson, they selected a defensive end named Dwight White.

"It took a lot of courage for Chuck to make that deal for Jefferson and even more when he traded off Richardson so quickly," recalls Art Rooney, Jr. "He could easily have kept Richardson around to make the Jefferson deal look better, but he quickly saw that Willie was over the hill and wasn't the answer to our problems. When we sat down for the next winter's draft, we wanted that fourth pick we had gotten for Jefferson to be an especially good one because that was all we had to show for the deal."

As the draft continued, the Steelers snatched additional names that would be found on their Super Bowl roster four years later, tight end Larry Brown, safety Mike Wagner, and, with the choice they got from Miami for DeMarco, another defensive lineman named Ernie Holmes.

In addition to these Super Bowlers, the Steelers signed as a free agent from that graduating class a starter at safety, Glen Edwards, and three other players who provided useful service before the championship year: Mel Holmes, Ralph Anderson, and Craig Hanneman. Anderson, a defensive back, was the dividend from Miami for Richardson.

The story of how the Steelers happened to draft White isn't as dramatic as the policy decisions involved in the selection of Greene or the happenstance surrounding L. C. Greenwood. But it does show something about how scouts work.

White had been well regarded by Pittsburgh scouts and their BLESTO combine the spring before his senior season. Art Rooney, Jr., had visited the campus in Commerce, Texas, where Coach Ernest Hawkins called White "one of the best athletes I've ever had here." During the next fall, the Steelers collected additional reports on his progress and saw some film. "He wasn't a little terror like Joe Greene, but he held his own out there and I liked his techniques," Artie recalls.

Young Rooney made a mental note that White reminded him of another top prospect of that year, Joe (Turkey) Jones of Tennessee State, who eventually would go in the second round to Cleveland.

Jess Thompson, a legendary scout who died of a heart attack while helping the Jets prepare their final plans for the 1975 draft, had been watching White for several years as Southwest talent hunter for BLESTO. He had an easy way with players, especially the blacks. One spring he told White that he had a pro future, but there were a few areas in which he could stand improvement. Outwardly, White appeared extremely skeptical; in fact, "he looked at Jess like he was crazy," according to one observer. But the next fall, when Thompson returned to the campus, White not only was doing some of the things the scout had suggested, but he came over to thank him for the advice.

Thompson wrote in his reports that White reminded him of Cedrick (Nasty) Hardman, a former teammate of Joe Greene's at North Texas State. Hardman had been drafted number one by San Francisco the previous year and already was developing into an outstanding defensive end.

As the fourth round progressed and it came time for Pittsburgh to exercise its Baltimore pick, White's name was well up on the priority list. "Thompson saw a great athlete in White and I saw a great athlete in White, so that's why we decided to draft him at that point," Rooney recalls.

White's reaction was similar to that of Joe Greene two years earlier. Pittsburgh, Pittsburgh? White remembers thinking.

"It was the furthest thing from my mind, no exaggeration. I knew there was such a thing as the Pittsburgh Steelers but that was all I knew about them. The only Pittsburgh player I had ever heard of was Joe Greene."

When White reported to the Steelers, there had been a major change in the coaching staff. Walt Hackett had died that spring and Dan Radakovich was recruited from the college ranks to take over his duties. At the time "Bad Rad" was defensive coordinator at the University of Cincinnati, but he had made his earlier reputation turning out all-America linebackers for Penn State.

From his Penn State days he was familiar with much of the Steeler personnel and their problems. He studied films and came to a firm decision: "Our defensive line is too slow to win with."

Coming off the 1970 season, the Steeler front four consisted of Ben McGee and Lloyd Voss at the ends and Joe Greene and Chuck Hinton at the tackles. McGee and Hinton were thirty-two, Voss was twenty-nine. He and McGee had each played seven seasons in the NFL, Hinton had been around for six. Greene was the baby, and in his first two years he had benefited from playing beside the steady and experienced Hinton.

As usual, the rookies arrived at training camp first, and White was immediately impressive. "He wanted it very badly," Chuck Noll recalls. "He had great desire to play and a great desire to do everything just right. He'd get angry with himself when he made a mistake."

Radakovich also was impressed with White. He could run the forty in 4.9 seconds, which was important on the pass rush, and he had the strength to handle the run. Plus he had an extremely rare combination of intelligence and *kamikaze* spirit. He was punishing the other rookies. (Because of his quickness and some background in that area, there was some thinking that White also might be a prospect on offense. But because he had been playing defense for most of his college career, he was started off there and, of course, never had to be moved.)

Still Radakovich hesitated. He had no personal pro background and he feared that he might be overrating White. The late-summer waiver lists are filled with the names of rookies who starred against their peers but then came down to earth with a thud when matched against the late-arriving veterans. However, after the veterans reported to St. Vincent, Radakovich's first impression was vindicated. White was a player.

At the same time Rad also started to like the way a third-year guy named L. C. Greenwood could move. There was a huge speed gap between White and Greenwood and the two veterans. What to do about it?

Radakovich's plan, which he sold to Noll, was simple. L. C. Greenwood and Dwight White would become the defensive ends, right now. White, as mentioned, had impressed immediately as a prospect, and Noll figured that Greenwood was ready to pop. As long ago as late winter, when Steeler publicist Joe Gordon was preparing the team's early prospectus, Noll had told him, "Go a little stronger on L. C."

Voss and McGee then would be moved inside, where their lack of speed would not be so critical, to compete with Hinton at right tackle. (Hinton soon after was traded to the Jets.) Voss and McGee also would take an occasional practice turn at end to remain ready to move back outside if one of the youngsters should be injured or break down.

Some coaches like to ease their rookies into the lineup. Radakovich was impatient. There would be five exhibition games for the young bucks to learn their jobs, and besides, what did the Steelers have to lose?

In the Steelers' first exhibition game, White and McGee alternated quarters at right defensive end but in the second the rookie got in for only a handful of plays. "That's it, I'm on my way out," White decided, but actually the opposite was true. It was McGee who was getting his last shot. In game three, White was the starting right end, with Greenwood on the left, and he went all the way from there on.

Before long the rest of the National Football League was to become very much aware of Dwight (Mad Dog) White, including a young Patriot quarterback named Jim Plunkett, who once ended up with two black eyes and a bloody nose from one collision with the Steeler end's forearm.

"Actually, back in Dallas, I was a big sissy," White once told Pittsburgh sports writer Phil Musick.

White was born in Hampton, Virginia, and lived there until he was almost fourteen. His father, originally from Dallas, had moved east to attend Hampton Institute, a famous old black college. "The school followed the old Booker T. Washington idea of teaching black people to assimilate into the social structure by becoming useful to it by doing things with their hands," Dwight recalls with some bitterness. "My father majored in industrial education, but by the time he finished the course, his skills were obsolete. Being a security-minded person, he became a postman in Hampton."

Eventually, G. L. White was able to arrange a transfer

back to Dallas, and this is where the development of Dwight White as man and football player really began.

"The community I lived in wasn't one of the best communities in the world," White reminisces without fondness. "It was a really raunchy black community with holes in the streets and junkies and winos all around. I went to an all-black school and I can't say too much for it as far as counseling or teaching you things you could identify with. Some of the teachers tried, but most of them just wanted to get away at four o'clock."

White to this day doesn't think kindly of Dallas. Although he visits there and calls himself a Texan, he considers his home to be Pittsburgh, where he lives in a high-rise apartment in the Squirrel Hill section. The living room, dominated by a statue of a black Jesus and stereo components, is furnished in modern athlete-Spartan, as compared to the modern athlete-oppulent of a Joe Namath or Walt Frazier.

"I never really liked Dallas," Dwight says today, "and I don't like it now. It is so pitiful for a city of the size of Dallas and as pretty as it is to have such an ugly inside. It's really black inside. It's a situation that I just can't deal with because I have too much on my mind. I'm too busy trying to succeed to deal with people who have such trivial things on their minds like just being black or white. They worry about that here in Pittsburgh, too, but there's more movement here. If it's not straight ahead, at least it's in circles, at least they're juggling it around. People in Dallas are stagnating.

"I respect Dallas for being one of the biggest business centers in the United States. There's a tremendous amount of wealth there and living conditions are fine and people are aggressive. But I guess the thing is that I stayed there for a while and all I had was bad experiences. All I had was bad luck."

One of those unpleasant experiences could have revolved around that fall afternoon when his parents took him downtown to see President John F. Kennedy ride through the streets of Dallas. It was only after they returned home that Dwight learned the reason for all those sirens after the motorcade had passed.

White has two younger brothers but he grew up as part of a huge family. His father was one of fourteen children, his mother one of twenty-one. There were literally cousins by the dozens.

As the eldest, White grumbles, "I was the one who got all the discipline, I was the one who always got whipped, I was the one who had to go to work." Dwight White is not one to forget, whether it's having to go to work in a grocery store after school or being held by some rookie tackle in an obscure exhibition game years before. "You beat me in a game and I'll get you; someday I'll get you," he says. He's never forgiven Bob Vogel, the veteran Baltimore tackle, for beating up on him one game when he was a rookie and then retiring after the season before Dwight could get a rematch.

The family lived in a government housing project in Dallas and young Dwight ran with the neighborhood gangs.

"We used to go and steal and I'm embarrassed to tell you what," he confessed one rainy afternoon in his bachelor apartment as he smoked steadily despite his recent bout with pneumonia. "We used to steal clothes off people's clotheslines. Three or four of us used to go through the projects on warm summer nights and pick out what we wanted. Socks, pants, and stuff. We had all the clothes in the world."

The moon-faced lineman has an almost unnoticeable scar on his neck, just below the chin.

"We were stealing one night and this lady cut the light on and we broke and ran. I was running through the back yards, ducking under the wire clotheslines, but one of them was broke and sagging a little. It was night and I couldn't see it and this time I really got clotheslined. It knocked me down, cut my breath off, but I got up and kept on running 'cause I was scared.

"We did a lot of stuff like that, took money from the smaller kids, the things that can eventually make you end up in jail. One of my old friends is in the pen now and another has been and is out, but he could be back in now, too. We never stole wheel covers and stuff, and when the other guys went downtown to shoplift I stayed home. I wanted to go, but I was scared.

"I'd smoke when I got away from the house and drink beer. I was a regular run-of-the-mill little hoodlum," White relates with a little chuckle.

But in the ghetto jungle, every victimizer is also a victim. He still remembers with guilt the night his favorite pet dog was killed following him across the street as he and the gang were going to steal pomegranates from the tree in a neighbor lady's yard. "I cried and I cried and the first thing I thought was that she had been killed because I was doing wrong," he says, still shaken a dozen years later.

"I got in a lot of fights in school because I was always the biggest even though I was younger than most of them," he went on. "There were always older kids in school who wanted to get a reputation and they'd pick on me because I was big. I got my money took and I'd lose a lot of fights and get hit in the mouth and I'd be scared to come home some ways because of the other gangs."

White went out for football in junior high and was cut. His pride was stung. He did not try the sport again until the spring of his junior year in high school. By this time he had blossomed physically and the coaches had been pleading with him to join the team. He did, and played tight end. "Until then I was a lady's man. I'd rather walk them home from school than stay and practice football. But after I began having some success in football I discovered that I was that much more popular on campus," Dwight says with a broad smile.

At this point, Dwight hadn't organized his goals in life. Though bright, he had little interest in attending college. Maybe it was because he saw how little advanced education had done for his father. But his parents were pressuring him to continue his schooling and a couple of local colleges were impressed enough with his football future to try to make it easier for him.

One of these was Prairie View, an all-black school. The other was East Texas State, one of the recently integrated white colleges, which was located in Commerce, a small town about sixty miles northeast of Dallas. White signed a letter of intent with both schools.

The modern East Texas campus impressed him. He could see his face in the shining floor of the student union building. He'd never seen anything "so fine," but still his first decision was to enroll at Prairie View. However, when it came time to report early with the football team, Dwight was still working at his summer job as a lifeguard and hadn't even begun to pack. East Texas drills didn't begin for three more days. By that time he would be ready. East Texas it was.

The decision opened up a whole new world for White, although it took him many years to come to terms with it.

The trauma is best related in his own words:

"When I left high school I went from an all-black community, unexposed to anything else. All my experience was there [in the ghetto], which I had never left and where I was drowning in my own spit. Then I went up to East Texas State. It had maybe thirteen thousand students and only thirty-five or forty were black and eighty percent of them were athletes. I had gone from one extreme to another, and that's when I began to become aware of how unexposed to life I had been.

"I had so many misconceptions about both ways of life and I wasn't that happy about the college I was at, either. There were some positive things, but my overall experience was bad. You'd get hurt and coaches would say things like 'Roll him off the field.' Yet I don't hold anything against the coaches now because I know they've changed. I even go down and see 'em now and then.

"It was tough relating to the white students. How could you when they had this Old South Week every year and guys would walk around in those Confederate uniforms? The teachers weren't that cooperative and the town was just a little racist town where sixty percent of the people worked at the college.

"I know some people had worse experiences, but for me to come out of the situation I'd come out of in Dallas, and then to go back to it on weekends and in the summer—well, the future looked dim, dim, dim.

"My last years in college I was very bitter. Most of my friends were gone and I didn't socialize much. I didn't want to be around anybody and I had no girl friends. I thought about how if somebody had made me apply myself in high school how much better a student I'd have been; how if I'd started out earlier in athletics how much better an athlete I'd have been.

"When I got drafted by Pittsburgh, I started to wipe East Texas State out of my mind. I went back there to work out that summer and it was my way of showing them they hadn't done a thing for me. I was telling them I appreciate your scholarship because it allowed me to get an education; I mean an education about people. Because if I'd stayed in the ghetto, I'd never have had a chance to find out about you and how you operate and the world I'm going to have to contend with the rest of my life. I thank you for that, but at the same time my thanks are bred out of bitterness."

White can easily call up that early bitterness and frustration, although much of it has been exorcised in recent years. His feelings are understandable. He is a gifted young man in mind and body, but he came so close to missing out. He knows he could have ended up still standing on a Dallas street corner, or maybe working for one of his uncles who owned a "joint" in the ghetto. The fear of what might have been can breed bitterness.

An interesting aspect to all of this is that Greene and White both attended the same kind of school in the same general area of Texas. Greene was there a couple of years earlier when integration was still an uncomfortable novelty, yet his memories are not bitter. However, White's college term included periods of greater campus unrest. John Carlos, the militant black-gloved Olympic runner, was at East Texas then, and White recalls how a black athlete's revolt was "utterly crushed" by the administration. White says he was not part of the proposed boycotts. By that time he had already set his mind on a professional career and he refused to let any cause interfere.

Bill Nunn, the Steeler scout, is familiar with both schools. Nunn used to be sports editor of the weekly *Pittsburgh Courier*, one of the nation's leading black newspapers. One of its better-known promotions is the naming of a Black College All-America team every year, a roster that is must reading in every pro scouting department. From scouting prospects for that team, Nunn became a part-time aide with the Steelers and eventually a full-time scout. He's been visiting campuses like North Texas and East Texas for years, looking at them through the same eyes as a Dwight White or a Joe Greene.

"In those days, the two schools were pretty much alike. Their campuses and student bodies were similar and the racial situation was the same," he says. "I'd say the difference in the way they remember college is the difference between Dwight White and Joe Greene."

The experience, however, worked to help White grow, which he readily acknowledges. When he first got to college he was there "to get my parents off my back." His early friends were upperclassmen and he watched as they were drafted by pro teams. Sam Walton, a tackle, was a third-round draft choice of the Jets and played in the Super Bowl. Rich Houston a year later was picked by the Giants to be a receiver. Glamorous big-city teams had sought his pals. "I got to get drafted, too," Dwight decided, but still his goals were superficial; a car, money in his pocket, a nice apartment.

During those last years at college, though, Dwight says, "I started to rearrange my values."

Speaking of himself and the other three members of the Steeler front four, he says, "All of our values have changed and now we can see beyond our noses. We all had weak and flimsy ambitions, if we had ambitions at all. But now we see the sky's the limit if you do the best you can.

"Respect is really important," he continues. "Back then, everybody had to struggle, it was a struggle just to survive. Now it's a struggle to be number one and we must constantly be setting goals for ourselves. Success, you know, is one of the biggest medicines for people coming out of the situation like the one we did. A little success sometimes goes a long way, and if you never have any success you'll never do anything good."

Today Dwight White takes correspondence courses from East Texas to complete work on his degree in history. He also works for the federal Department of Commerce in a program to ease top minority high school students into career on-the-job training during the summer so that they'll be experienced and valuable job prospects when they graduate.

Yet he also likes to drop by the Steeler personnel office to threaten Bill Nunn and the rest, "When I finish playing I'm gonna become a scout and do one of you out of your job."

In addition to a changed awareness of the world, Dwight White brought two things out of college, a huge ugly scar on his left knee and that attention-grabbing nickname. There's some relation between the two.

White went to East Texas as a tight end and played that position as a freshman. However, the first spring practice before his sophomore year, he suffered a knee injury that could have cost him his leg, and possibly his life.

The East Texas coach liked to try his players both ways during spring practice, and White was working out at linebacker on a muddy field when the quarterback sprinted out in his direction and then cut back. White stopped in his tracks and was standing there with his legs planted apart when the blocker crashed into him. "I almost died from the pain," he remembers, as the knee gave way.

As White tells the story, a trainer slapped a cast on his knee and he hobbled around the campus for two weeks with nothing more being done. When the knee failed to improve, he was sent to a doctor, who discovered that ligaments and cartilage had been torn. Surgery was performed.

White went home to Dallas with a new cast on his leg, but the day he was scheduled to return to school the pain became worse and he returned to the hospital.

Again, let Dwight tell it:

"They thought it was just 'claustrophobia' or something, that I couldn't stand the idea of having my leg in the cast, but I told them the leg was swelling and so they cut a little hole in the back. When they looked in, they saw I had so many blood clots it looked like grape jelly. The incision had spread apart and the staples had cut through the flesh. The odor was unreal and the doctor's eyes got this big. He took the rest of the cast off and took his hands and mashed my leg and the blood just shot up. That's when I passed out and they took me up for another operation.

"What happened was that an artery had been damaged when I got hurt and it had given way. At first they couldn't stop the bleeding. They had these pails and they kept squeezing the congealed blood out. The doctors said I was very lucky. One of the clots could have got to my brain or, if the artery had given way when I was off someplace, I could have bled to death."

It was this treatment that helped create some of White's bitterness toward East Texas State. Unbelievably, though, through dedicated therapy, the leg healed and the next fall Dwight was out for the varsity. Coach Hawkins preferred another, more experienced tight end ahead of Dwight—naturally he's still angry about this, too—but he said, "You're too good not to be playing someplace, so we'll put you at defensive end."

White didn't have the greatest football background, anyway. One year of high school and another with the ETS freshmen. Defense was a whole new world. "I didn't know what I was doing," Dwight admits. "I couldn't 'read,' I couldn't 'key.' I had no idea about team defense. When the ball was snapped, I would go. Sometimes I'd make spectacular plays and sometimes I looked like an ass because they would run a play right where I'd just left from. One day I was really making some wild moves and the coach yelled, 'Dammit, why do you just run in there like a mad dog?' "

And that's how Mad Dog White got his name. It's stuck, though, because it so accurately describes White's style of play—"He is crazy out there," a Steeler watcher says—and because he does look especially fierce when he's playing without his dentures.

"The hardest I've ever been hit in my life, both times were by Dwight," Joe Greene recalls with a shudder. "He's just rough, like a bull in a china shop, and he'll tear up anything that's in his way. It's like he's got tunnel vision and he zeroes in on that one thing and anything that gets in his way, too bad. One time against Chicago, we're both coming at the quarterback and suddenly everything went black. He'd swung that forearm and the quarterback ducked and so he got me. You've got to watch out for White."

Over the years, White has had to refine his techniques somewhat. He's cut down on smashing quarterbacks in the face. That's an automatic penalty. "You can hit him low even after he's thrown the ball and usually they won't call it," White confides. "Still, it's the best feeling when you catch the quarterback from the blind side and really get a good lick on him. I gotcha! Then you're rushing and you see he really wants to get rid of that ball and he's ducking and you know you've got him. Some of them you can tell when they're intimidated and that's a good feeling, too."

When he gets to the quarterback, White loves to fling him to the ground with a flourish.

Like his other front four colleagues, White becomes infuriated when blockers try to hold him illegally. Only more so, perhaps. His teammates fear someday he will go beserk and hurt somebody. He admits that once he got so angry at being held that "I could have literally snatched that guy's arms out of his shoulders if I didn't know I would go to jail for it." On another occasion he said he was tempted to "bite the guy's ear off." It's not complete hyperbole. He has been seen kicking and slugging in the pit and once he was thrown out of a game for kicking at the Giants' Bob Tucker. White insists the tight end swung at him first with an unnecessary elbow, unnecessary, that is, because the play was going the other way. White indicates he might have been more sympathetic if Tucker had needed to block him to make the play work.

Sill, despite these fierce, aggressive attitudes and the bluster, there's a certain insecurity in Dwight White; a fear of being made to look bad, an inability to accept a loss or the tag of "second-class ball player." Nunn and others who know him well feel much of White's conversation is a cover-up and Dwight himself admits, "I have an ego problem."

Joe Greene spotted this at once. "When Dwight first got here, I thought he was a linebacker, he was so fast, but I don't think he was really sure of himself," Joe recalls. "I kept trying to convince him that he had the team made, to get that burden off his mind, to relax him. Even now he's still convinced they're going to trade him."

Fortunately, White arrived, just as Radakovich and the Steelers were changing their philosophy, and he helped make the transition easier with his outstanding play. Soon he and Greenwood could, in Joe Greene's words, begin to "relax and play."

The Steelers, for the first time in years, were competitive in 1971. They blew a lot of close games, but still managed to finish with a 6-and-8 record, second best in the AFC's Central Division. It was their best record in eight years.

For the first time, the front four began to develop an identity. Some fans and writers began to refer to them collectively as the Steel Curtain. The basic group that would crush Minnesota in the Super Bowl three seasons later was on the grounds . . . more or less.

6

Fats

Dwight White still remembers the first time he met Ernie Holmes.

Soon after the 1971 draft, the Steelers invited all their rookies to Pittsburgh so they could see what their scouting department had wrought and to get the youngsters launched into the preliminary steps of their professional careers. They would be weighed, measured, charted, tested, and, where necessary, put on weight and diet programs so they'd be trim and strong for training camp. "We want our rookies to make it," Chuck Noll says.

The new players were quartered in the massive Pittsburgh Hilton Hotel, part of the city's new Golden Triangle downtown showpiece on the river across from the stadium. They had been drifting in from various college stations around the country and many of the black players from the South and Southeast had gathered in one of the larger rooms.

Dwight White was a late arrival, but with a "Hey, man, what's happening?" and a few introductions the glib lineman was soon part of the crowd. He thought it strange that another home boy from Texas seemed somewhat withdrawn. White and Ernie Holmes had shaken hands when introduced and then they had parted in the crowded room. Throughout the evening, White was conscious of Holmes staring at him through small, close-set eyes, even though he knew they had never met before that day.

Finally, through the natural flow, Holmes and White found themselves face to face. Up to this point the conversation in the room had been light and friendly, if somewhat agitated. All the rookies were nervous. As he and Holmes stood together, though, the mood changed. The shorter, stubby Holmes belligerently spat out the words. "Yeah, fat boy, you know you're gonna have to leave here," he snarled. "There's not room for more than one of us here."

For Holmes, who had played in college at over 300 pounds and whose own nickname from boyhood had been Fats, to call anybody "fat boy" was kind of presumptuous, and White was definitely put off by his approach. It was completely out of tune with the rest of the evening. Wow, where do you come from? Dwight thought.

White is no dummy, however, and he quickly realized what was happening. "Ernie obviously had gone down the list of draft choices," White explains, "and he thought I was a defensive tackle and that I was going to be his competition. He saw I had been drafted in the fourth round and he hadn't been picked until the eighth and so he was starting to sell Wolf tickets [sic] to me with this psychological intimidation. We both knew only a certain number of people can make it at any position.

"He kind of ran away with it, though. He's telling me that I definitely have to leave and that I might as well get back

on the airplane right now. It really shook me at first and I
pulled right away, but then I put it right out of my mind."

The Steelers kept the rookies in town for a couple of days
and on the final afternoon Ernie Holmes came up to Dwight
sweet as pie and began talking as if they were long-lost
cousins from Texas who'd just been interrupted as they were
chatting on the party line.

"Of course, he'd found out that I was a defensive end, and
since he was a defensive tackle, I was no longer any threat
to him," White recalls with a laugh. "He was too embarrassed
to admit anything or apologize, and he probably figured I
hadn't picked up on why he'd talked to me like that the
other night and why he was changing so suddenly. So I said,
'I know why you did all that; forget it,' but he didn't say
anything. He just laughed. Later I learned that was just
Ernie."

After the indoctrination camp, Holmes went back home to
Texas, but he returned to Pittsburgh a full month before
training camp to start getting in shape. He was accompanied
by Bert Askson, a Texas Southern University teammate who
had been drafted by the Steelers as a linebacker the year before but had failed to stick.

They worked hard that month as Holmes followed orders
to lose some thirty pounds and he continued a wicked pace
through two-a-days at St. Vincent. He cut his speed for the
forty-yard dash and he got his weight down to the requested
265 pounds, but it was a struggle and the severe recent weight
loss showed in workouts. Although he did everything the
coaches asked, and more, he had too far to go at this point
to play in the NFL. He did not have White's speed afoot or
quickness of mind, and, with the big front four changeover

that involved moving Ben McGee and Lloyd Voss inside, the Steelers were loaded with tackles. In September, as the season opener drew near, Ernie Holmes was cut.

The decision was a tremendous blow to Ernie's fragile ego. He had staked all on making the team and now he was being told he had failed.

But not entirely. The Steelers were not giving up on Ernie. Once he cleared waivers they wanted to keep him on their taxi squad as a future prospect. Holmes refused. Taxi squad pay was about $1,000 a month. "Humph, I can make more than that working back home on the docks," Holmes boasted to his teammates.

Dan Radakovich, the defensive line coach, tried to persuade Holmes that he had a future with the Steelers. He pointed out that the team was cutting some experienced defensive linemen and sending them home. Ernie was being kept around ahead of them.

"Look, I don't want to sit around all year waiting for somebody to get hurt. These guys are my friends," Holmes said stubbornly as he packed his gear.

There were several reasons why Holmes elected to leave the Steelers at this point. For one thing, he fully expected to be claimed on waivers, or at least picked up as a free agent by some other NFL team.

For another, he was already becoming hemmed in by the marital and financial problems that would lead to his breakdown two years later. He needed more money than the standard taxi salary to fulfill some of the obligations he had already begun to incur in overly ambitious attempts to help his parents, as well as to care for his own young family. Even if he left now, he would get to keep his bonus. Also, he had been

away from home for several months. He missed his two in-
fant sons and he was homesick. "There was a lot of pressure
on me because I was the successful one in the family," Holmes
admits now, although he's probably aware that much of this
pressure was self-imposed, "and I was already having problems with my wife."

The major reason, though, was probably simple embarrassment. Fats Holmes had fully expected to make the team. On
occasion he had even half-jokingly boasted that even Joe
Greene's job wasn't safe. There had been that psych-out
threat to Dwight White the night they first met, and now
White was enroute to becoming a starter and it was Holmes
who was "gonna have to leave here." The humiliation was
complete. "His whole life was becoming a pro. I think he
was just too embarrassed to stay," Dan Rooney says with un-
derstanding.

And so Ernie Holmes returned to Jamestown, Texas, a
small community north of Beaumont near the Sabine River,
which separates Texas and Louisiana. Ernie grew up there on
the family's forty-five-acre farm as the second oldest of eight
children while his father worked full time in a nearby local
pulp and paper mill. It was a grandfather who started calling
him Fats.

Jamestown, as Ernie recalls it, was a close, mixed community where blacks and Cajuns from Louisiana lived side
by side. "It was one of those places where my momma is your
momma and your momma is my momma," he says. Scout Bill
Nunn recalls it as a spot where even the smallest child had
an identity. "Wherever you went, they always knew you as
the Holmes boy and where you were from," Nunn says. Identity would become very important to Ernie Holmes in the

future, but in his early youth there were always plenty of farm chores to keep him busy.

Like most of his fellow members of the Steel Curtain—a phrase Ernie likes more than the others—Holmes started out playing sandlot football. His father preferred that he play in the band rather than for the high school team. Emerson Holmes was afraid that Ernie and his older brother would get hurt, but he finally consented when he learned the boys had been sneaking off to practice football anyway. "Okay, you can play," he grumbled, "but if you get broken up I'll shoot you like they do a horse."

As Ernie won fame as a high school football player, he received dozens of college scholarship offers. After all, he stood 6'3" and weighed 295 pounds as a high school senior, and he was agile enough to see occasional duty at fullback. He must have been an awesome high school fullback, once he got going. All the black schools in that area sought him, as did some of the nation's major universities up north, including Michigan State. Bubba Smith of nearby Beaumont was just finishing a great career at Michigan State.

But Texas Southern, a predominantly black school, was in Houston, only some 150 miles way, and, as Ernie puts it, "My father forced me to go there so he could watch me play, which he did only two or three times while I was there." On second thought, he amends "forced" to something like "strongly suggested."

Holmes had his problems at Texas Southern, a modern university in the heart of downtown Houston, most of which centered around how he was being handled. There also was a bloody racial incident there his freshman year. At one time, he says, his father had to "threaten to put his big hands on me" to keep him from quitting. He started as a sophomore at offensive tackle and was moved to middle guard on defense his junior and senior years. He also met his wife and was married at Texas Southern, and that's where she now lives, in Houston, with their children.

Ernie believed in the conspiracy theory on why he wasn't drafted until the eighth round. He feels he was the equal of such members of his draft class as Tody Smith of Southern Cal, Bubba's brother, and Isiah Robertson, who played at nearby Southern University. Both went in the first round. Instead, he says, "I didn't go until the eighth because I found out later somebody told people I weighed two hundred and ninety-five pounds and ran the forty in eleven seconds."

The fact is, all the scouts seem to agree that Holmes, despite his denials, did play at over 300 pounds at times in college, and people in the Steeler personnel office snickered when Bill Nunn reported that he thought the beefy tackle had "quickness."

"Quickness? At three-hundred pounds?" they asked.

And Nunn would reply that inside all that fat, quick feet and an agile body were struggling to escape. If Ernie was willing to pay the price and lose the weight, they would see it, too.

In another apparent contradiction, Holmes says that despite the earlier problems, Ernie had his former college coach act as his agent when he first signed with the Steelers. He feels he was taken here, too, and he says of his former representative, "I learned a lot from that experience and I appreciate him learning me, but I wish he'd left me with some of the finances."

Still, as best as can be determined, Holmes signed pretty

much the standard rookie contract for an eighth-round draft choice, a bonus of perhaps $5,000 and a base salary near $20,-000 with some incentive clauses that could bring it up. The year of his breakdown he was making $30,000 a year. It apparently wasn't that Ernie threw his money away on cars and clothes; the consensus among friends is that he tried to do too much for too many people close to him too quickly.

Ernie's father was back in the middle once his son returned from his first Pittsburgh camp. They argued for hours. "Don't you know what you're turning down?" he'd ask.

"Yeah, I realize," Ernie would reply. "But they just don't recognize me as an individual. I'd just be wasting my time to try to prove myself again."

Eventually Emerson Holmes got on the phone to Pittsburgh. He explained to club officials his son's disappointment. "I've tried to instill pride in my family and that's why it's hard for Ernie to accept second best," he told them. He hinted that Ernie probably would be receptive if someone called to show that the Steelers cared.

About this time, Art Rooney, Jr., was returning to Pittsburgh from a scouting trip that had kept him away for a couple of weeks. He was shocked to hear of Ernie's defection. He had been high on Holmes from the beginning and grew more fond of him after he visited Texas Southern to sign him to his first contract.

Holmes had been so anxious to prove that the Steelers had made a good choice that he ran a couple of forty-yard sprints, even though the Steelers had plenty of clockings on him, and then, as Rooney and his son, Little Fats, looked on, he challenged Julius Adams, a TSU teammate, to a wrestling match. Adams, also a defensive tackle, had been drafted by the New England Patriots in the second round, but Holmes quickly pinned him. "He killed him!" Rooney exclaims, still impressed today. "Here was an eighth-round draft choice turning out to be stronger and quicker than a second-round choice!"

Later Rooney and the full coaching staff would be impressed by Holmes's dedication to diet as well as his good-humored willingness to do "anything we asked of him in training camp."

On his return, Rooney asked what had happened to Holmes and the coaches told him the full story. They also indicated that they wouldn't mind having him back, if only in a taxi capacity.

Would Artie call the temperamental tackle? Artie would, and did. "Look, we want you back," he said simply. "We think you can be a great football player. Don't blow your chance."

Artie modestly insists that Ernie would have heeded anyone who called from Pittsburgh; he just happened to be the one who was tapped. But the fact is, he had been a great booster of Holmes from the beginning and his eagerness to learn what had happened to Fats may have set the wheels in motion. On top of this, the moody Holmes considered Art Rooney, Jr., a friend, and he very well might not have listened to anyone else. As the Steelers flew home from Oakland after assuring their berth in the Super Bowl, Holmes grabbed Artie in the aisle of the jet and gave him a huge hug. "You're the guy who brought me back," he said emotionally.

That call, of course, was all Ernie had to hear. He began packing his bags to return to Pittsburgh.

Other related events were occurring in other NFL cities

to make a place for Ernie Holmes, although none of it would be exactly simple.

About this time, a promising rookie defensive tackle with the Jets, Scott Palmer, was racked up badly in an automobile accident in which a teammate hit a pole. A friend who was handling some of Ernie's affairs at this point heard the news report and headed off Holmes at the airport.

"Hey," the breathless friend asked, "did you hear the Jets' prime defensive tackle has had an accident and you're the prize they're going to pick up? Where you going, anyway?"

"Back to Pittsburgh."

"You got to be lying. Wait here and let me call the Jets."

"Can't. I promised to come back."

"Well, break your promise!"

"Can't," said Ernie Holmes and he headed out the door to catch his plane for Pittsburgh. (There also were reports that Kansas City was trying to find Ernie at this point as well.)

Still another confrontation awaited Holmes as he walked into the Steeler office on the other end of his flight. Chuck Hinton was there with his bags packed.

"You turkey, you had this all planned, didn't you?" he snapped at Holmes, who was slightly dumfounded.

"What you mean?"

"They're shipping me out to New York and they're bringing you up here, that's what," the usually taciturn Hinton continued, and then he asked, "Hey, why don't you go on up to New York?"

All Holmes could reply was "I'd love to," but he was only twenty-three and Hinton was thirty-two, and the Steelers knew what they were doing.

As it turned out, Ernie never officially made even the

Pittsburgh taxi squad that year. Since he had already cleared waivers, the Steelers felt they could safely stash him on what some NFL executives refer to as the "hide" squad. At that time, NFL clubs were allowed to have forty active players under contract, plus seven more "futures" in reserve, the taxi squad. Most kept several supernumeraries around, though, shadowy figures who jumped at the sign of a camera, league official, or visiting scout. Their job was to practice and keep a low profile. The Steelers, among many others, were frequent practitioners of this maneuver, and they've been fined several thousand dollars for it by the league office. Near the end of the season, Holmes was requested not to dress for the official team picture.

It took a complex series of transactions the next spring so that Holmes could break his cover. First the Steelers signed him to a new contract, then they had to put him on no-recall waivers. The Patriots claimed him in a prearranged deal and sold him back to the Steelers for cash.

Holmes, ignoring this charade, was determined to make it the second time around. "If I leave this time, they'll have to drag me off the field," he vowed.

However, the full year of semiactivity had taken its toll. Holmes may have been a ghost player, but his figure was hardly ghostly at the end of the season. His weight had crept back up to 285 and when he returned to momma's cooking he quickly ballooned to 303.

He says this is the most he ever weighed, but he didn't remain there for long. He went on an immediate crash diet and for the next few months allowed himself only one meal with meat each day. He also ate a few eggs and drank lots of water. He took vitamin pills. In one week he lost twenty-two pounds.

He didn't just diet, however. He ran as if he were training for the Olympics morning, noon, and evening for a total
of ten miles. When he got back to 280 and no longer feared
being seen by the Steeler coaches, he returned to Pittsburgh.
Training camp was still three months off, but Fats wanted to
be ready when they opened the gates. He continued to diet
and run; around the Carnegie-Mellon University track nearby,
up and down the stadium steps, up and down the hills
and dales of Squirrel Hill, where he lived. Sometimes he'd
run wearing a ski mask in hopes Steeler fans wouldn't recognize him. He could hardly be inconspicuous.

When he reported to camp in July he was back down to
260. He says he ran "some of the slowest forties in my life
at camp, but when they got to the three hundred fifties, the
guys were calling me antelope."

Qualifying for the Olympic quick-weight-loss event and
ten-mile run didn't exactly carry with it an automatic berth
with the Steelers, however. Early in training camp he suffered a pinched nerve in his neck that affected his right arm.
Holmes is a physical-style tackle. He says he leaves the finesse
to the man beside him, Joe Greene. The head slap is one of
his favorite weapons, second only to the head butt, a technique he says he borrowed in college from offensive linemen
who used this spearing approach on him.

"It's offensive line technique," he explains. "You dip, hit,
raise, and then hit in the numbers, and I've found I can
get a lot of respect from an opponent doing it this way. It's an
intimidation piece and ruins the guy's concentration, too.
Also, you don't have to wait for him to make his move, you
go to him. You do all this gypsy stuff and you get your legs
broke. I don't have time to get my legs broken. Being low
and straightforward gets me to the job and just as fast."

Afraid to let the coaches know he was hurt, Holmes remained silent, and so the staff was mystified at his poor performance. They figured he had regressed since his rookie year, which often happens, and there was talk that if he didn't come around he would be cut.

But, as one coach points out, "Fortunately for Holmes, when he was struggling we didn't have to cut anybody at his position, and by the time we did, he had come around."

Holmes kept on practicing just as hard through his painful ordeal, taking his usual extra workouts most afternoons with guard Sam Davis. When the coaches finally discovered that he had been hurt, they admired him even more for his Spartan spirit. His strength was awesome.

The only fault they could find besides inexperience was the way he went all-out in every drill, even when they didn't want him to. Sometimes the offensive line just wants to work on its timing and footwork. If one defensive lineman comes crashing in as if it's Sunday afternoon at the Super Bowl, it ruins the whole exercise. But Ernie Holmes always feels he has something to prove, even if it's a light break-a-sweat Saturday drill. "If you don't want to be out here, don't come out here," Holmes snarls at the cursing guards, and *wham!* the head slap to the ear holes of the helmet and *bam!* the helmet in the gut and the bells are ringing once again.

As the season drew near, the Steelers had more decisions to make. They could not carry four tackles and Joe Greene was set as one, so that left three bodies for the remaining two spots, McGee, Voss, and Holmes. McGee and Voss had each played nine years, but Ben at thirty-three was three years older. Holmes was completely unproven. On the trading mart, Voss would bring the best price, and so he was dealt off to Denver for an eighth-round draft choice.

The Steelers decided they would alternate McGee and Holmes alongside Greene.

For most of the season, the two players saw duty on alternate series. McGee, according to friends, didn't mind the arrangement. He knew his legs were gone and he seemed to like the idea of grooming his replacement.

The first game of the season, he had to give Holmes a valuable lesson that friendship must end at the sideline. The Steelers opened against Oakland and McGee/Holmes were matched against left guard Gene Upshaw. Upshaw was from Texas and Holmes had known and admired him for years. "A nice person, I kind of dig his style," Holmes said. Trouble was, Holmes played in awe of the Raider guard.

The first time he came out after his first series, though, Holmes found McGee waiting for him. The veteran chewed him out. "Look, you gotta hit that sucker upside the head," McGee snapped, and Holmes realized that he would be humiliated if he did not. "I realized then that you got to get respect for yourself, that it's a job," Holmes said as he recalled how he "started to capitalize on the things Ben was telling me and jolted the guy on the side of the head."

(Incidentally, the head slap is legal, although in recent years it's supposed to be limited by the rules to one blow per charge. Offensive linemen laugh hysterically when you tell them this.)

Holmes played well that day and the Steelers went on to make the playoffs, but Ernie was impatient with his role. "I thought I was professional stock even then and not a second stringer," he insists, but by the end of the 1972 season he

was playing virtually the entire game. When the season
ended, Ben McGee announced his retirement.

A first-string job was waiting for Ernie Holmes. He had a
playoff check in his pocket. He should have been sitting on
top of the football world.

7

The Immaculate Reception

Chuck Noll was concerned as the 1972 campaign drew near, although, of course, he kept his apprehension to himself. This would be his fourth season as Steeler coach and he had yet to produce a winning record. A considerable number of promising rookies had been making the team each year, but was this because they were so good or because the veterans were so bad?

He was wondering, and he knew it was only a matter of time before the players—and eventually the Rooneys—would be wondering, too. Players are worse second-guessers than fans.

"We had to have a good year in 1972," Noll admitted as he looked back from the heights of Super Bowl success. "I felt that if we were going to lose, we could lose the football team from an attitude standpoint."

The parade of outstanding draft choices continued in 1972. The Steelers' first pick was Franco Harris, the strong, silent fullback who had played most of his career at Penn

State under the shadow of teammate Lydell Mitchell's gaudier statistics.

Three years earlier, Noll had made a stand in favor of drafting Joe Greene. In Harris's case, he allowed himself to be persuaded by his scouting department. Noll had favored drafting Robert Newhouse of the University of Houston. But after many long arguments he finally deferred to the personnel department, which pointed out that Harris was just as fast as Newhouse, and bigger. Noll has final say over the draft but he reluctantly agreed to go along with his scouts, who proved correct. While Harris was setting Super Bowl records for Pittsburgh, Newhouse, drafted in the second round by Dallas, had still not won a regular job.

Over the next four rounds, the Steelers also drafted offensive tackle Gordon Gravelle, tight end John McMakin, linebacker Ed Bradley, and defensive end Steve Furness, all of whom would see Super duty in New Orleans.

And then, down in the eleventh round, they made what in the next few years would develop into their most controversial pick of all, a spindly black quarterback from predominantly black Tennessee State, Joe Gilliam.

There also was one additional new recruit in the class of '72 who would play a major role with the front four. Dan Radakovich, on the staff for only one year, left to become defensive coordinator at the University of Colorado. (He would return two seasons later as offensive line coach.) To fill Rad's spot, Noll hired George Perles, a defensive assistant at Michigan State.

Although he had no pro background, the down-to-earth Perles became an instant hit with his defensive linemen.

"He's a million and a half, he's a doozy," says Ernie Holmes.

"The maximum," chimes in Dwight White, who calls Perles "the fifth man on our defensive line."

The object of this affection is a stocky native of Detroit of Lithuanian ancestry who spent two years in service after finishing high school and then enrolled at Michigan State. He won a starting job as a two-way tackle his sophomore year, but then tore up his knee and never played again. However, he remained in school, eventually earned a masters degree, and then started the long coaching road in high school.

An astute football man, he's lauded by his players for pregame preparation. Holmes says, "He gets us so ready, when we go out there it's like watching a movie."

Perles also has a colorful way of turning a phrase. Here are some Perles-isms:

On Joe Greene: "He'd cut off his nose to help a friend."

On Minnesota coach Bud Grant, known for his conservative, unemotional approach: "You can't all go around and wear brush haircuts and have ice cubes in your veins." To Perles, all players who react well under pressure have "ice cubes in their veins," an intriguing image.

On the toughness of his defensive line: "Intimidation is part of our game. They could be the greatest street-fighting front four of all time. They don't get any lip service."

On pro athletes' emotionalism: "They're not always cool, calm, and collective."

On a disappointing loss to Houston en route to the Super Bowl: "Very flustrating."

On getting overcome with one's own importance: "You've got to make sure your head still fits in your hat."

The affection his players have for George Perles is reciprocated.

"I didn't play professional football and I anticipated problems coming here because of my background," he says. "But these guys proved to be very coachable. I worked with Duffy Daugherty at Michigan State and he used to say people can tell how you feel about them. Even a dog can tell. Well, they know how I feel about them and I can tell that I'm accepted in return. We have a great relationship.

"These guys could do well if you just threw the ball out there and played without practice. They have great ability and without great ability you're just whistling Dixie. But, in their case, they are getting all they can out of their ability. They bat damn close to one hundred percent.

"They're all goom-boddies [sic], too. They have great compassion and feeling for each other and for Coach Noll and the team. They take great pride in being unselfish. They think about it, they are aware of it, and they talk about it. They're all potential great businessmen, I think, and I call them young executives right now."

Perles, of course, has worked intimately with the front four longer than any other single coach. "They all have excellent but different ability. They complement each other," he says, and this is how he appraises the individual members of his Steel Curtain:

"Start with L. C. He's six-six, a two-hundred-thirty-eight pounder, and in most circles he would be too thin for defensive end. He might be a linebacker like Ted Hendricks [a 6'7", 218-pounder known as the Mad Stork]. But he has that four-point-seven speed and he gives us a dimension other teams don't have. He helps us batting the ball down and is valuable going after plays on the other side and coming off on screens. He uses more finesse in his technique, and when

Franco Harris (left) and Joe Greene carry coach Chuck Noll off the field after Super Bowl victory. *(Steeler photo)*

Here they are, the Steel Curtain (from left): Dwight White, Ernie Holmes, Joe Greene, L. C. Greenwood. *(Steeler photo)*

THE MANY FACES OF JOE GREENE

One of the Mean Greene at North Texas. *(North Texas State photo)*

Sideline concentration *(Steeler photo)*

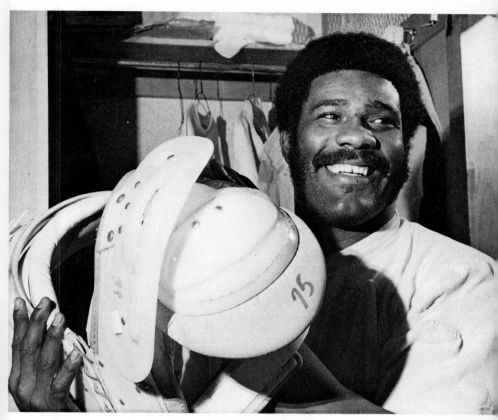
This goes on the shoulders, right? *(Steeler photo)*

THE MANY FACES OF
L. C. GREENWOOD

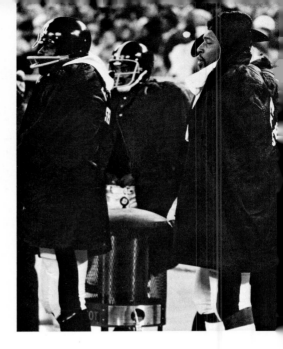

Trying not to be too cool.
(Steeler photo)

Hollywood Bags, who else?
(Steeler photo)

Hot work. *(Steeler photo)*

The pain of football. Dwight White rehabilitates knee after undergoing surgery in college. *(East Texas State photo)*

THE MANY FACES OF DWIGHT WHITE

Not always an angry man. *(Steeler photo)*

"I'll get him next time." *(Steeler photo)*

Before the arrowhead. *(Steeler photo)*

Ready for combat. *(Steeler photo)*

Pointing the way. *(Steeler photo)*

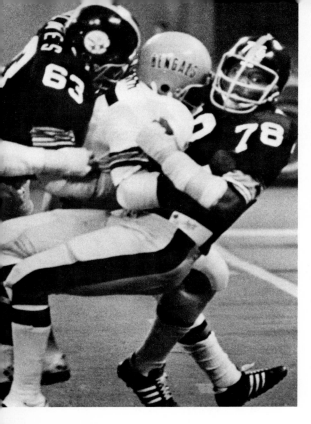

How to make a Bengal go Meeaow. Ernie Holmes (left) and Dwight White supply the crunch in 1973 game. *(Steeler photo)*

Even though he's gotten off his pass, Baltimore's Marty Domres knows he's gonna get it from Joe Greene in this 1973 pre-season game. *(Steeler photo)*

The Dwight White forearm poised for action. Steelers vs. Cleveland, 1973. *(Steeler photo)*

Getting the defense ready. Chuck Noll flanked by Joe Greene (75) and Ernie Holmes (63). Jack Ham is No. 59. Sub quarterback Terry Hanratty (5) in background. *(Steeler photo)*

Strategy talk. Assistant coaches George Perles (left) and Woody Widenhofer with Joe Greene. *(Steeler photo)*

After recovering fumble against Cleveland in 1974 game, Joe Greene prepares to lateral off to J. T. Thomas, who runs it in for winning touchtown. No. 63 is Ernie Holmes. *(Steeler photo)*

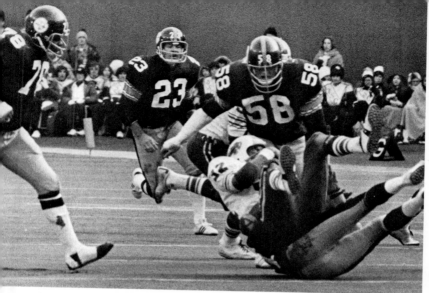

Down goes O. J. Simpson in NFC playoff. Dwight White (78), Mike Wagner (23), and Jack Lambert (58) ready to help out. *(Steeler photo)*

Sack goes the Raider. Joe Greene drops Ken Stabler for loss in AFC title game. *(Steeler photo)*

Dwight White's discomfort is obvious as he tries to work out at midweek before the Super Bowl. He had to return to the hospital. *(UPI photo)*

Joe Greene on his back, a rare pose. *(Steeler photo)*

Above: L. C. Greenwood (68) belts Dave Osborn as ball flies loose to set up safety against Vikings in Super Bowl. Below: Mike Wagner signals the two-pointer as Jack Lambert wraps up Fran Tarkenton after Dwight White (not visible) made the actual play. L. C. Greenwood (68), Ernie Holmes (63), and Joe Greene (75) are right there, too. *(Both UPI photos)*

Fran Tarkenton's view all through Super Bowl. Here comes L. C. Greenwood. *(UPI photo)*

The man behind it all with his rewards. Art Rooney, holding game ball and Super Bowl trophy, accepts congratulations from NFL commissioner Pete Rozelle (left). *(UPI photo)*

he slips someone, he's usually wide open. He's not only different from the other three, he's different from most other linemen. He's a Jekyll and Hyde. Normally when you have someone with his speed and quickness, he's not tough enough to play in the trenches, but he is the exception.

"Then you have Fats Holmes. He is the other extreme, six-two, two-seventy-five. He's the typical defensive tackle, strong. Normally a person with his height limitation and thickness is handy against the run and operates parallel up and down the line but has trouble rushing the passer. But, for some unknown reason, this guy has the agility and quickness to get to the passer. Normally when our other guys make the rush, he comes on like the second wave and gets the sacks when the quarterback is chased out of the pocket. He helps us on draws because he's usually a step or two behind Joe. Instead of a parallel wall, he makes it look like a graph.

"Dwight is really a true combination football player, equally good against the run and the pass. He's six-four, two hundred and fifty, and has ideal height, weight, and speed, a picture player on paper. He's also a very emotional, aggressive player who stimulates the other people up front. In games, if anyone tries to take advantage by holding or if a play is not called right by the official, he brings it up and gets the other three fired up.

"Joe is a superstar. He is as quick as most light fellows and as strong as anyone. His greatest attribute is that he can take his massed body, coil it up, and come off in the first two steps like nobody ever has in this league. It's hard to measure the way he can unload with mass strength, force, and quickness.

"He's also a great leader by example and probably de-

mands by his own effort and leadership more respect than
any other player in the league from officials, coaches, and his
teammates. I saw it when we were coaching in the Pro Bowl
in 1972. People like Deacon Jones, Willie Lanier, and O. J.
Simpson came out of their way to say hello. Even officials do
it through sheer respect.

"Thank God he has a pure attitude, otherwise he's the
kind of player you'd have to get rid of because he is so strong.
He's a team player. He couldn't care less about individual
sacks, but he gets a great thrill out of what his teammates
do."

The Steelers opened the 1972 season at home against Oakland, and at that time the bitter rivalry with the Raiders had
not yet developed. Pittsburgh won, 34–28, but although their
fans and many outsiders were elated, some skepticism remained inside the organization. "It was such a flukey thing,"
one player remembers. The Steelers scored their first touchdown on a blocked punt and Bradshaw had to run for two
scores himself. Then, in the last quarter, the Steelers barely
survived a twenty-one point Oakland rally. Noll warned, "I
know all about opening victories. My first season we started
out one-and-0 and ended up one-and-thirteen."

Pittsburgh's next three games were on the road and the
Steelers lost two of them. Thus after four weeks they were
2–2 and worried.

For game five, however, Noll made an important decision.
To this point Franco Harris had been used only sparingly.
In one game he didn't carry the ball once. His total stat sheet
showed only twenty-six carries for seventy-nine yards. But
Noll now felt he had to unleash his number one draft choice,
and Franco, whose father, a black career soldier, had brought

home an Italian war bride, responded like a thoroughbred who's been prepped all year for a major stakes race. He carried nineteen times for 115 yards and a touchdown in a 24–7 rout of Houston. The Oilers' only touchdown came on a blocked punt and the front four had one of its big days. Houston quarterback Dan Pastorini was sacked five times for forty yards in losses, leaving the Oilers with a passing net of zero yards.

The following week Harris gained only twenty-seven yards in eleven carries as Pittsburgh crushed New England, 33–3, and Jim Plunkett was sacked six times for seventy-two yards in losses. But the next Sunday he took off again and for six straight games gained one hundred yards or more, tying an NFL record previously set by the great Jim Brown. In each of those games Franco scored at least one touchdown.

A fan club known as Franco's Italian Army was founded by the owner of a Pittsburgh bakery and they showed up at games wearing khaki helmet liners and waving Italian flags. By this time the whole town had Steeler fever. Almost every player had a fan club. The most colorful next to Franco's Army was known as Gerela's Gorillas, in honor of place-kicker Roy Gerela. Gerela had been claimed on waivers from Houston just before the 1971 season, the only player obtained by the waiver route to appear on Pittsburgh's Super Bowl roster, incidentally. He's a Canadian who learned about football while living with a sister and attending high school in Hawaii. He kicks soccer style. The leader of his fan club showed up for all games wearing a gorilla suit—what else?—and they would all sit together in the end zone and hang out signs designed to psych out the opposing kicker.

After their 2–2 start, the Steelers won five in a row, their longest winning streak since 1958. Fourth victory in the run was 40–17 over Cincinnati, avenging an earlier 15–10 loss to the Bengals in which Horst Muhlmann had kicked five field goals for the winners. L. C. Greenwood, playing in pain with a damaged ankle, enjoyed a big afternoon against Cincinnati and his teammates awarded him the game ball. "They said it should have been a Purple Heart," L. C. laughed.

Victory number five was 16–7 over Kansas City, still considered one of the NFL's class teams that season. The Steelers then lost at Cleveland, 26–24, but came right back with a 23–10 victory over Minnesota, another powerhouse. At this point they were tied with Cleveland for first place in the AFC's Central Division. But the next week they got the Browns at home and broke the tie by mauling them 30–0. Dwight White, who had played most of the season with painfully bruised knees, got into a screaming, cursing match with several Browns players as they left the field. Pittsburgh's defense had been so dominant, Cleveland never advanced into Steeler territory after the first quarter.

The Steelers clinched a sure spot in the playoffs as at least a wild card team by beating Houston in the next to last game of the season, 9–3, as Joe Greene enjoyed one of the most spectacular games of his career. He blocked a field goal, forced and recovered an important fumble, sacked the quarterback five times, and made six unassisted tackles.

"It was the best performance I have ever seen by a defensive tackle," said former Houston coach Lou Rymkus, who was scouting the game. Joe was named Defensive Player of the Week by the Associated Press.

More meaningfully, he was given the game ball by his teammates, and he had to treasure Andy Russell's presentation speech on the plane ride home. "After much consideration," Russell said, "we decided to award the game ball to a guy who is so outstanding that much of the time his play is taken for granted. We are giving the game ball to Joe Greene."

In the final game of the season at San Diego, the Steelers wrapped up the division championship, their first in forty years of trying, by beating the Chargers, 24–2. Before the game, Frank Sinatra was officially inducted into Franco's Army, and he still sends the team a good-luck telegram before big games. The victory marked the seventh game and third in a row in which Pittsburgh's defense did not allow a touchdown. The Steelers thus closed with four straight victories, including the last two on the road, and their 11–3 record was by far their best ever. Only once before, in fact, had they won as many as nine.

During this final stretch, Ernie Holmes was getting almost all the playing time at right tackle ahead of Ben McGee.

At one time late in the season, the Steelers had been enraged by a local television commentator who charged that they would always be losers, that when you put a good player in a Pittsburgh uniform he magically became a bum.

The Steelers of old may have subconsciously played this way, but during the season of '72 their attitude began to change. They began to believe in themselves.

John Dockery, a former Jet who had played in New York's Super Bowl victory, joined the Steelers early that season. He was a cornerback from Harvard, an incongruous combination, and he showed up just as Lloyd Voss was being traded to Denver. So the Steelers just gave him Voss's old locker, right in the middle of all the offensive and defensive linemen.

"When I came to Pittsburgh, I expected to see this Mean Joe Greene as some kind of mad animal sitting in the corner eating railroad ties or something, and it wasn't that way at all," Dockery recalled one day. "I found this Joe Greene to be a gentle, nice, friendly fellow.

"When I came there, there was a locker open among the defensive linemen, and so they slapped me down right in the midst of all those gorillas—and I mean that affectionately," Dockery continued. "There were some offensive linemen there, too, and we had all these big characters with the higher numbers while all the other defensive backs and so-called 'skill' players were on the other side. I was like a dwarf among giants.

"But because of that I got to know them all and to appreciate them and their sense of humor. Every once in a while, though, Ernie Holmes would come over and start horsing around with Joe Greene and they'd begin to wrestle. It was like two huge dinosaurs grappling in prehistoric times. They weren't trying to hurt each other, but it was frightening. You'd pull your chair back into your locker and hope they didn't roll in your direction. Joe didn't do anything special to make me feel at home when I joined the team. He just did it by being Joe."

Dockery found the Steelers and his front four lockermates "very interested in someone who had come from New York and who had played in the Super Bowl."

As the Steelers approached the playoffs, Dockery began to wear his Super Bowl ring. "You could see the gleam in their eyes and you knew that someday they'd have one, too," says Dockery, who was released by Pittsburgh on the last cut before the Steelers' Super Bowl season.

Dockery was somewhat surprised to learn of the players' interest in Joe Namath. "I guess they saw him as a symbol of success, a symbol of the radical who could flaunt it," Dockery remembers. "They were always asking questions about him, almost like adolescent hero worship. It was strange to see these superstars—and Joe Greene at the time was a superstar—asking those questions about Joe Namath. I considered them at the time on the same level and yet here was Joe Greene looking up to Joe Namath."

Dockery, as a recent pickup, was able to look on the team with a somewhat detached attitude, and his respect and affection for his new teammates are obvious. "All the time I was a member of the defense, I was in awe of it," he says.

Because of his unique position, Dockery also was able to notice the change in Steeler attitudes. "That first year we made the playoffs we beat some very good teams and that's when the players began to feel that every game they went out there they were going to win," Dockery says. "That was the feeling we had with the Jets, even during the bad years after the Super Bowl. We just knew we were going to win. I don't think they had that feeling in Pittsburgh when I got there, but things started to change when we beat Kansas City and Minnesota. The guys started to say, 'Hey, these are the superpowers in the league, and if we can beat them, we must really be good.'"

Noll agrees completely. He also points to those games, Kansas City and Minnesota, as turning points for the Steeler Suicide Syndrome. Also important were those one-sided reversals of losses to Cincinnati and Cleveland, who are in Pittsburgh's division and who therefore must be faced and conquered twice each season, plus the two closing victories away from home. All three Pittsburgh losses had been on the road, a long-standing Steeler failing.

Fortunately, the luck of the draw and their position as division champion dictated that Pittsburgh would be the home team for the first two rounds of the playoffs. Their opening opponent was Oakland, champion of the Western Division.

The Raiders were hexed from the beginning, starting with their arrival Friday afternoon before the game with quarterback Daryle Lamonica sick and unshaven from fighting the flu. There was no question of Lamonica's staying in the night before the game. After the Raiders' short workout, he stopped off at the front desk to pick up some medication and headed straight for his room. He looked awful.

Events at that pregame workout should have told the Raiders something, too. The Oakland team is paranoiac and obsessive about secrecy. Once before a playoff game in Oakland two league officials were setting up the press box when a Raider official ordered them from the stadium. "Nobody watches the Raiders practice," the functionary declared. This, of course, was ludicrous, since practice the day before a game is not exactly a Broadway dress rehearsal. It's basically a light warmup to loosen muscles cramped from a plane ride, to get the players acclimated to the field, and to break up the day so they can't spend too many consecutive hours drinking beer. They usually do calisthenics, play catch, and work on the kicking game.

The Steelers operate one of the most open teams in the NFL, and when the Raiders showed up this wet afternoon at Three Rivers Stadium they immediately had to set to work to clear the area. Newsmen, grounds crew, everybody not connected with the team or dressed in silver and black was being chased. Then somebody looked up into the stands. An attractive feature of Three Rivers Stadium is the plush Allegheny Club, where members can sit and dine and drink and watch the game, baseball or football, from their tables. That afternoon there were perhaps one hundred people in the Allegheny Club. Enjoying their annual Christmas party, and with a full view of the field and the Raiders' workout, was the Pittsburgh Steeler office staff!

Al LoCasale, the Raiders' administrative assistant who had been busy shooing people off, threw up his hands in frustration. For the first time in memory, non-Oakland reporters and other outsiders watched the Raiders practice. They learned nothing.

Oakland's travails continued through the night. The Raiders were quartered in the downtown Pittsburgh Hilton Hotel, and a local radio station had announced plans for a giant pep rally several blocks away. As the rally grew in intensity, the Steeler fans decided to march to the Hilton, where their yelling and screaming hopefully would upset and intimidate the visitors. So far, so good.

The crowd was in reasonable good humor when it arrived at the plaza in front of the hotel, but it didn't stay that way for long. John Madden, the Raiders' massive head coach, is an inveterate lobby sitter, or stander. The night before a game, he'll camp in the lobby for a few hours to watch the world go by. It's one way to pass the time—and check on your players.

Madden is a huge figure. A knee injury kept him from playing tackle in the pros, so you can figure how big he is, and since then he's put on weight. Through the plate-glass windows of the Hilton lobby, he was a highly visible and recognizable figure to the crowd as he stood there looking out with folded arms. Despite the Raiders' reputation for intrigue, Madden is a basically open man and one of the brightest young coaches in football. He was probably just curious as to what was going on, but to the crowd his stance suggested defiance. The mob, numbering several hundred and with no place to go, began to get ugly. They surged forward against police lines, cursing at Madden. A bottle crashed against a second-floor window and an older police-man slipped and fell off one of the small stone walls around the entrance. "One of our guys has been hurt," the now nervous officers whispered down the line.

Into this tense scene came two of Oakland's reserve players, tight end Bob Moore and linebacker Greg Slough. They had been to the movies, and now they wanted to get back into their hotel before curfew. There was a back entrance, but they didn't know this. "Nobody's going in," ordered the police, and Slough backed off. Moore, however, was stub-born. "I'm a player, I'm with the Oakland Raiders," he insisted. "Sure, sure," the police replied, for Moore, from Stanford, has a babyish round face and in street clothes really doesn't look like a football player. Moore pushed forward but the police line stood firm. Somebody cursed. The police, more and more edgy, started swinging. Moore was beaten to the ground and then, according to his account, was man-handled more in the paddy wagon en route to the station house.

When the Raiders finally got him out, Moore was a mess. He announced plans to file a lawsuit against the Pittsburgh police, plans on which he followed through although at this writing the case was pending. He showed up for the game the next day with his head swathed in bandages. He could barely get his helmet on, but he did play.

The Raiders were naturally enraged, but the Steelers took it in stride. They already were angry at Oakland for a delay in the exchange of game films, a standard Raider ploy. "At least we've got the police on our side," they shrugged.

The game itself was tough and defensively brilliant, with the Steelers holding a decided edge most of the way. The first half was scoreless, but Pittsburgh got some offense going in the third quarter and moved close enough for Gerela to kick an eighteen-yard field goal. The guy in the gorilla suit beat his chest.

The fourth quarter was more of the same, a Steeler defense led by a front four that refused to yield and a twenty-nine-yard field goal by Gerela produced a 6–0 lead with four minutes to play.

By this time, Madden had replaced the ailing Lamonica with a young left-handed quarterback named Ken Stabler. Gunning one pass after another, Stabler moved the Raiders down to Pittsburgh's thirty. Again he dropped back to pass, but, as had been the case most of the game, Pittsburgh's pass coverage was perfect. And the pass rush did not allow Oakland quarterbacks time for someone to break free. Dwight White had been shaken up and Craig Hanneman, a rookie, was filling in for just that one play. As Stabler danced around in the pocket, looking vainly for a receiver, Hanneman smelled the sack. He forgot about the cardinal rule of containment and came zooming in to throw Stabler for a loss. He also forgot that Stabler was (a) left-handed and (b) an accomplished runner. Since he was a southpaw, he would find it easier to scramble in Hanneman's direction. Quarterbacks, except for the knee cases and geriatric marvels like Sonny Jurgensen and George Blanda, are just naturally more nifty than most defensive linemen, who outweigh them sixty or more pounds. Stabler spotted Hannemann coming and sprinted around him. The alley was wide open. Stabler easily scored and Blanda's extra point gave Oakland a 7–6 lead with 1:13 left to play.

It was Same Old Steelers time and more than fifty-thousand fans in Three Rivers Stadium slumped collectively in their seats. I, incidentally, was covering that game for the *New York Daily News.* I had been writing a running account for the early editions, and when Stabler scored I began to prepare my bulletin lead based on a probable Oakland victory. The lead would then be transmitted to New York when the final gun sounded. My account, however, was to be interrupted in midsentence, as we shall see. Today that aborted lead is framed and hanging in the office of Ed Kiely, public relations director for the Steelers.

The fans weren't the only Steeler boosters who figured the game was lost. Art Rooney, Sr., seldom visits the locker room after games, except, as he qualifies, "when we're on the road and I've got to pick up my suitcase."

On this occasion, though, he thought he should be there to greet his beaten players when they came off the field. He wanted to be there to share their disappointment and to let them know that he was still proud of them and what they had achieved and how they had played on this chilly afternoon. After all, they were the first Steelers in forty years to win a championship of any kind. He appreciated that. He wanted them to know it.

The Raiders kicked off and Pittsburgh set up at the twenty for its last offensive shot. They were eighty yards and seventy-three seconds from defeat in a game they had dominated except for one broken play.

As Terry Bradshaw completed two short passes to move Pittsburgh out to its forty, Art Rooney was locked in his thoughts on the elevator down to the dressing rooms below the stadium.

By now Bradshaw was throwing desperation passes to get Pittsburgh at least into field-goal range. He tried three and all three fell to the Tartan Turf incomplete. Fourth down and he had only one more chance. On the sidelines, Chuck Noll sent in rookie receiver Barry Pearson with a play. Pearson would be the primary receiver. If the pass was successful, there would be time to attempt a field goal.

The Raiders, however, figured Pearson would be the primary target, and they held him up at the line of scrimmage so he could not run his pattern. Bradshaw looked frantically downfield, trying to separate the swirling shapes and images, seeking another open receiver. Once he was almost caught for a loss, but he ducked under the Oakland tackler and scrambled first left, then right, buying precious time. His running backs were drifting downfield, looking for an open spot. Suddenly Bradshaw spotted Frenchy Fuqua, seemingly unguarded at the Oakland thirty-five.

Bradshaw let the ball go and Jack Tatum, Oakland's ace free safety, left his man, tight end John McMakin, and sped toward the Pittsburgh halfback. It was a long pass and Tatum had time to get there. He thought he might have a chance to intercept, but Fuqua positioned his body to protect the ball and so Tatum decided his best shot was to lay a solid lick on Fuqua just as the ball arrived to make him drop it.

Tatum, Fuqua, and the football all came together at the same instant in a brutal collision that sent Fuqua flying. Out of this mass the ball ricocheted back upfield toward the line of scrimmage. The trajectory was downward, and when the ball hit the ground, the game would be over for Pittsburgh. On the sidelines, some of the Steeler players saw the fourth-down pass falling incomplete and they started to compose themselves for the moment of defeat.

Suddenly out of nowhere came Franco Harris. Harris was supposed to stay in and block for Bradshaw, but then, as Terry scrambled, he headed out to provide a safety-valve opportunity in case the quarterback had nobody else to throw to. When he saw the ball heading downfield to Fuqua, he tried to catch up to the play to block for his teammate. "He was hustling," Chuck Noll would say of Harris after the game. "Good things happen to those who keep hustling."

As the ball bounced away from the collision, Harris thundered toward what he knew was the Steelers' last chance. In full stride, he picked it off at his shins at the left hashmark of the Oakland forty-two. After Tatum appeared to have broken up the pass, the Raider defense froze for an instant. That gave Harris the advantage he needed in the desperate foot race. He headed for the sidelines, his face a mask of determination, and with long strides galloped into the end zone. One of the officials tentatively threw up his hands to signal touchdown with five seconds to play.

Art Rooney was waiting in the dressing room when he heard the muffled roar from outside. "What happened, what happened?" he demanded. A clubhouse aid checked outside. "We scored a touchdown!" he yelled.

"But where are the players?" Rooney asked moments later. If the Steelers had scored a touchdown with only seconds left, the game should be over. How come no overjoyed players were clumping into the dressing room? "There's a question about the touchdown," Rooney was told, and the seventy-year-old Steeler owner settled down for what he later termed "the longest wait of my life."

The question was whether Harris had made a legal catch. Two offensive players cannot touch a forward pass in succession. If the ball had bounced off Fuqua into Harris's hands, it would be ruled an incomplete pass. But if at any point it had touched Tatum, the catch was legal.

Players from both sides milled around in disorder. Spectators, who had erupted in wild elation a moment before, sat sullenly in their seats as officials huddled on the field. There was a crowd of fans around the end zone. Suddenly referee Fred Swearingen, in charge of the crew, headed off to one of the baseball bullpen benches where there was a phone to the press box. Swearingen wanted to speak to Art McNally, a league supervisor of officials who was at the game. At that time there was an NFL rule forbidding officials to talk to reporters after a game. Under pressure from the Pro Football Writers of America, and largely as a result of this incident, it has since been modified. According to McNally and Jim Kensil, another NFL official who monitored the call, Swearingen and McNally discussed only the possible rulings. Swearingen, Kensil related, wanted McNally to know that he was aware of the "double touching" rule but that the officials felt the ball had bounced off Tatum. Mc-

Nally then agreed that in that case, their ruling of a legal touchdown was correct.

To this day, however, despite disclaimers to the contrary, suspicion exists in many quarters, especially in Oakland, that Swearingen knew McNally had seen the play shown in replay on the press box TV monitor and he was seeking a supporting opinion when he placed the call.

Whatever, the issue was resolved and agonizing minutes later Swearingen threw up his arms in a definitive gesture and the touchdown was allowed. Gerela kicked the extra point and, seconds after the ensuing kickoff, the Steelers raced off the field with a 13–7 victory.

The first Steeler in the dressing room was punter Bobby Walden, the oldest man on the squad. He grabbed Rooney in a bear hug and swung him around. "We won! We won!" he yelled.

Later Tatum would say he had no awareness of having touched the ball and Fuqua would only smile vaguely when asked if the pass had really bounced off him. He seemed to enjoy the mystery. The Raiders for months insisted it was an illegal catch. Given the force and direction of the ricochet, it appeared to me in the press box that the ball must have hit off a piece of Tatum's equipment, possibly a shoulder pad, which would account for his not feeling it. Fuqua might have had a hand in there, too, which would account for his hints that he might have touched the ball. If both touched it, though, it was a legal catch.

The Rooney family, without being sticky, is strongly and openly Catholic. Art and his wife, Kathleen, attend mass every morning. In addition to his brother, Father Dan, a platoon of priests is always in evidence wherever the Steelers appear as a group. Now they had won their biggest game on a miracle play clouded in mystery.

There was nothing else to call it but the game of the Immaculate Reception.

8

Generations of Losers

The city of Pittsburgh went wild, practicing its own peculiar brand of civic celebration, which consists of a great deal of boozing and brawling in the streets. Previously this kind of frenzy had been reserved for baseball triumphs, but tonight the football fans got a taste. Until this season the Steelers had never won a championship of any kind, and now they had achieved their first playoff victory in history on one of the most spectacular, yea, miraculous, plays the sport had ever seen.

The Immaculate Reception victory truly symbolized the Steelers' turn-around, and to understand the celebration one has to understand the strong ties between this city and its ball club. The Steelers are Pittsburgh born and bred. They are as Pittsburgh as the Rooney clan that brought them to life. They are almost an anachronism in this day of absentee corporate-type write-off ownership by carpetbaggers who travel from town to town seeking municipally built stadia, tax benefits, and fat television contracts.

And Art Rooney, the patriarch, recognizes this. "It was

more fun before the big money came," he once complained.

Rooney was born in 1907, the oldest of eight children of a prosperous Pittsburgh saloon keeper. He grew up in an area of Pittsburgh known as the Ward. He still lives there, too, although the neighborhood has considerably deteriorated since his wife, Kathleen, purchased their five-bedroom home for $5,000 during the Depression. Mrs. Rooney, incidentally, had been brought up across the street from this home. The Victorian-style house is only a short walk from Exposition Park, where the Steelers and the baseball Pirates originally played their games before the construction of Forbes Field. Today, opulent Three Rivers Stadium stands on the site of old Exposition Park, across the river from downtown, and Mr. Rooney still walks to the office most days that he's in town. "I guess that's why I'm so close to the players," he jokes. "I live only five minutes from the stadium, and whenever the lights go on I go down to see what's happening."

The saloon was the hub of the neighborhood in those days, and young Art and one of his three brothers, Dan, later to become a Franciscan missionary, early in life became addicted to the leading extracurricular activities surrounding their father's establishment, sports and politics. ("It was a good saloon," old-timers recall, "no women allowed.") The boys boxed, played football and baseball. One summer they followed a carnival around western Pennsylvania and nearby Ohio. The carnivals usually featured a professional prize fighter to challenge local yokels in the ring. The local strong boys got a dollar or two for every round they lasted with the "champ." In this case, it was easy money for the adept Rooneys. They cleaned up—until the carnival barred them.

Art went to college at Duquesne, Georgetown, and Washington and Jefferson, and boasts that he had once been sought as a football player by the celebrated Knute Rockne of Notre Dame. He won amateur boxing championships and was good enough to turn pro and smart enough to quit. The Chicago Cubs signed him to a baseball contract, but his arm went dead while he was still in the minors. He was usually the star player as well as sponsor of various semipro football teams.

In politics, Art only once ran for office himself, as registrar of wills in Allegheny County. He swept all the precincts in the Ward but lost overall in a close race, probably because he confessed in campaign speeches that he didn't really know what the duties of the office entailed.

However, he served for many years as Democratic ward heeler in his home neighborhood, a job whose duties he understood very well. You took care of your friends and neighbors and on election day they presumably would reciprocate. Roosevelt's New Deal, with its social reforms and welfare programs, eventually made the old-fashioned ward heeler obsolete.

Rooney recalls that on any given Saturday night the phone would ring constantly at his home with calls from constituents who had been hauled into jail for being drunk and disorderly and for other infractions of that nature. "It got so I just left an envelope at the precinct house with enough money in it, and when I got these calls I'd tell the sergeant to take out whatever was necessary for the bond—ten dollars or twenty-five dollars—and to let the guy go when he felt better or when his wife or mother came to get him. Otherwise I'd have been down there a dozen times a night," Rooney remembers.

In sports, Rooney quickly branched out from participation to promotion. He was backing football and baseball teams and promoting fights. One of his early semipro football teams was known as the Hope-Harveys because "Hope was the name of the firehouse where they let us dress for games and Harvey was the name of our team doctor who took care of us for nothing."

Semipro ball in those days in the Pittsburgh-Wheeling-Canton-Youngstown quadrangle was of a pretty high caliber and the National Football League had not yet become the powerful monolith it is today. Rooney's semipros, recruited from such nearby schools as St. Bonaventure, Pitt, Washington and Jefferson, and Carnegie Tech, were pretty good. The state of Pennsylvania had blue laws that prohibited the playing of professional games on Sundays, but when that law was repealed in 1933, Art paid a $2,500 franchise fee and moved his Rooney Reds virtually en masse into the thirteen-year-old National League. He called them the Pirates, after Pittsburgh's baseball team.

Perhaps coincidentally, 1933 marked the beginning of the "modern" NFL. The season before, the Chicago Bears had defeated the Portsmouth Spartans, 9–0, for the league title in a game played indoors in Chicago Stadium. For 1933, sweeping rules changes opened up the game to include the forward pass as a major weapon and, at the suggestion of the late George P. Marshall, the league was split for the first time into two divisions and a playoff system was introduced. Whenever he talks about Marshall, an old friend, Rooney refers to him as "a reformed horse player."

Rooney quit drinking some fifteen years before his Steelers won the Super Bowl, but betting on the horses is one habit

he never kicked. Legend has it that he bought his NFL franchise with winnings from a major betting coup at Saratoga,
but that isn't true. He did break some of the books at Saratoga one week and this money did form the basis of the
Rooney fortune. But it all happened three years after Pittsburgh entered the NFL, in 1936.

In those days it was a lot easier to win big at the races.
Instead of parimutuel machines that constantly readjust the
odds as money is wagered, fans at the track placed their
bets with legal bookmakers on the grounds. If you bet when
the odds were four to one, that was the payoff, no matter how
much more money was wagered on a particular horse. Now,
with the state and the track taking a big piece of the betting
action off the top to further cut the odds for the horse player,
it's more difficult to make a big score. "The romance is gone,"
Rooney says sadly. One of his favorite bookmaker friends,
incidentally, was the late Tim Mara, owner of the football
Giants.

The most frequently mentioned figure for Rooney's winnings that week in Saratoga is $380,000, quite a princely
sum in those days of a national depression and low income
taxes. Rooney never mentions an amount, but some sources
hint it might even be higher. Art sent part of the money to
his brother Dan for missionary work and returned home
with the rest to tell his wife, "We don't ever have to worry
about money again."

Rooney later increased his stake by speculating in the com-
modities market, and he did well enough over the years not
only to bail out his own floundering team on occasion but
also to help needy friends within the NFL. Still a betting
man, he also races and breeds horses at his Shamrock Stable,

and, with his five sons running the various enterprises in person, the family owns a small string of harness and dog tracks through the East.

In 1940 the Pirates became known as the Steelers and Rooney took in a partner as a part of a complicated franchise swap. At the end of the season, Rooney "sold" his Pittsburgh franchise for $165,000 to Lex Thompson, a wealthy New York sportsman who was heir to tons of steel money and who had been an athlete of note at Yale. (Expansion franchises today bring $16 million.) Rooney then became partners with an old friend, the late Bert Bell, in the Philadelphia Eagles. That April, Bell and Rooney swapped franchises with Thompson, who opened up shop in Philadelphia. Except on paper for a few months in the off-season, Rooney never left Pittsburgh.

As best as can be deduced, old cronies Rooney and Bell set up this franchise swap and partnership so they could get hold of Thompson and his fresh money. Expansion for huge fees had not yet arrived as a popular fund-raising technique, and besides, this way they would not have to split with the rest of the league.

Several players also changed uniforms by lot in the switch and one of these was a young, little-used, one-eyed quarterback named Tommy Thompson. Thompson went from Pittsburgh to Philadelphia, another future champion quarterback discarded by the Steelers.

Bell, who had coached his own team in Philadelphia with disastrous results, also started out as Pittsburgh coach under the partnership with Rooney. He lost his first two games, was replaced by Buff Donelli, who lost five in a row, and then Walt Kiesling was brought back for the second of what would be three coaching terms. Kiesling had a great finish, 1–2–1.

In 1943, because of wartime manpower shortages, the Steelers and Eagles combined for one season under the nickname of Steagles. The next year, Pittsburgh and the Chicago Cardinals were temporarily joined for the same reason, and in 1946 Bell left the Steelers to succeed Elmer Layden as NFL commissioner. It was Bell who made the pro league rich and respectable.

Pro football in those days was generally low key. As late as 1946, Rooney can remember sending his team off to play exhibition games with precise orders to collect their fee from the other team before going out on the field for the second half. Once a new business manager disregarded this advice and got stiffed.

In those days, Art operated his team as a hobby. He saved most of his energy for the more serious business of horse racing. Today he regrets that indifference because the more he got into football, the more the loser's tag hurt, and the more he realized that with any kind of push the Steelers could have been winners long ago. "It was easier in those days," he says.

The highlight of this loose approach came during the two-plus years that Johnny Blood served more or less as head coach, from 1937 to 1939. Blood, a legendary running back with the Green Bay Packers and other teams, was known as the Vagabond Halfback. His real name was McNally, but he took his football name off a movie marquee advertising the film *Blood and Sand* in case he ever wanted to resume his college career. By the time he got to the Steelers, he was at the end of his career. His players didn't appreciate the way he would put himself into games at crucial times and kill off drives, and it got to the point where the team captain on the field would exercise his prerogative of refusing to accept Blood into the huddle.

Still, the players loved their happy-go-lucky coach, and, as Rooney recalls, "On most teams the coach worried about the players. With Blood, the players worried about the coach."

Once Blood missed the train back home from Los Angeles after a game. He wasn't worried because the then-Pirates had an open date the next Sunday, and so he stopped off in Chicago to watch his old Green Bay teammates play the Bears. Newsmen asked Blood how come he wasn't with his own team. "Oh, we're not playing this week," he replied nonchalantly, just seconds before the announcement of a halftime Pittsburgh score boomed over the loudspeaker. While Blood was wandering back from the West Coast, Rooney had scheduled a game in Wheeling. "You couldn't depend on John a whole lot," Rooney once told Myron Cope in dry understatement.

Frustration and bad luck marked the Steelers' operation. Once Rooney was about to hire Greasy Neale as head coach only to learn his old friend had a chance to land an assistant's job at Yale. "Pro football wasn't what it is today," Rooney says. "I told Greasy to take the Yale job." Neale, hired by Thompson, whom he had known at Yale, later would lead the Philadelphia Eagles to championships.

Rooney feels his best shot at winning in the old days came when he hired the legendary Jock Sutherland away from the University of Pittsburgh to be his coach in 1946. In their second season under Sutherland, the Steelers posted an 8–4 record to tie Philadephia for first place in the Eastern Division. However, they were shut out, 21–0, in a playoff for the title, and by the next season Sutherland was dead at age fifty-nine from a brain tumor.

"I always believe we'd have won a lot earlier if Sutherland had lived," Rooney maintains.

Yet it was Sutherland who forced the deal that Rooney says "broke my heart" when the so-called Dour Scot was unable to get along with perhaps Rooney's favorite all-time Steeler, Bullet Bill Dudley. Dudley was a triple-threat halfback out of the University of Virginia who was well able to carry the burden of Sutherland's single-wing offense. Dudley wasn't very big, just 165 pounds, and he wasn't very fast, and he didn't throw a very pretty pass. As Rooney says realistically, "If he walked out on the field today he wouldn't last two days."

But he could run, pass, punt, place kick, he was a terror on defense, and he played when hurt. In those days the pros played both offense and defense, and one season with the Steelers Dudley led the league in both rushing and pass interceptions. "Teams would order their passers not to throw in Dudley's territory," Rooney says.

Dudley came to the Steelers in 1942 as a number one draft choice, played a year, and then entered the service. He came out in 1945 and was there in '46 when Sutherland arrived. After one season, Dudley was ready to retire, and Rooney reluctantly traded his rights to Detroit. Bullet Bill played three seasons with the Lions and then finished up his career with the Washington Redskins. He is now a successful insurance man.

If Dudley has a rival in Rooney's affections, it is another

former star running back, Byron "Whizzer" White, whom the Steelers drafted number one out of the University of Colorado in 1938. White, a brilliant student, had a Rhodes Scholarship waiting for him, but Rooney persuaded him to play one season of pro football for the then magnificent sum of $15,800. "I don't remember what the eight hundred was for, probably exhibition games," Rooney says, and he points out that at this time most pros were getting between $100 and $200 per game.

Oxford reluctantly allowed White to enroll late, in January, instead of in September, so Whizzer could play his season with the Steelers. He led the league in rushing. When he returned from his studies in England he enrolled in law school and Rooney was convinced that White would never play pro ball again. However, the Detroit Lions were more optimistic. They bought White's contract from the Steelers and persuaded Whizzer to play two more years before the war finally ended his career. After a two-year layoff, White again led the NFL in ground gaining in 1940.

Today White is an associate justice of the United States Supreme Court, and he considers Rooney one of the finest men he has known. When Rooney was honored by the New York Chapter of the Pro Football Writers of America for long and meritorious service to the sport, White flew up from Washington to make the presentation.

"I knew from the beginning that no matter what he did, he was going to be a success," Rooney says of White. "He came as close to giving one hundred percent of himself as anyone I have ever known. We traveled by train in those days and White was always reading; and you knew they weren't cowboy books. But he was a regular guy, and on the way back from our last game of the season in New Orleans he threw a party for the whole team."

Rooney points to the signing of White and the hiring of Sutherland as two of several examples that show that the Steelers were willing to spend money to be successful, but it seemed as if the team almost suffered from a death wish.

Walt Kiesling was the coach in 1955 and he had definite ideas of what he wanted—mentally and physically—from candidates for the various positions.

One day Art Rooney received a letter from his twin sons, who were working as ball boys at the Steeler training camp at St. Bonaventure College in Olean, New York. They told their father about a rookie who was "the best quarterback in camp but the only people they let him throw to is us, and we're not on the team."

That quarterback, fired by Kiesling without getting into a single exhibition game because the coach thought he would never master the mental side of his position, was Johnny Unitas.

Chance helped dictate the Steelers' next coaching change on the eve of the 1957 season, at which point Pittsburgh, after twenty-four years of trying, had finished over .500 only four times.

Rooney had long admired Buddy Parker, a championship coach with the Detroit Lions, and suddenly the hard-drinking Texan was available. At a "Welcome Home" banquet two nights before the Lions' first preseason game, Parker stood up, announced that the team had looked so bad in training camp it didn't have a chance of winning, and so he was quitting on the spot. (Apparently he had misjudged his talent, however, because an assistant, George Wilson, took over and went on to win the NFL title.)

Parker was a certified football genius as well as a certified eccentric. Two weeks after Parker's bombshell, Rooney let Kiesling go—for the third time—and named Parker as head coach.

A year later, Parker brought in his old quarterback from Detroit, Bobby Layne, and together they provided Pittsburgh with some of its most colorful moments on and off the field. Layne, who played through '62, proved a superior leader despite his late-night habits, and Parker had only three losing seasons in his eight-year tour.

He did it, however, by trading off draft choices and young players for experienced veterans in the closing stages of their careers. George Allen has followed that route successfully at Washington, but he is the exception. Parker never did get his team into the playoffs. Their best season was 1962, when a 9–5 record was good for second place in the East and a trip to the Playoff Bowl in Miami, a consolation prize contrived for television. The Steelers lost there to the Lions, 17–10.

The Steelers were 7–4–3 in 1963, but the next season they slumped to 5–9 and the Rooneys were getting edgy about Parker's erratic and temperamental approach to the job. Dan Rooney was moving more and more forcefully into the management end of the business, and he became increasingly disturbed as whim and whiskey seemed to be the basis for so many Parker personnel decisions, especially after losing games. By this time Dan had been given operational control of the team by his father in a program to provide more professionalism in the operation. He put a stop to one of Parker's postmidnight trades, at least until they could look at it again in the sober light of day, and the infuriated Texan offered his resignation virtually on the eve of the season opener. Mike Nixon, an assistant, replaced him for one year.

At this point the Steelers officially set their course to catch up with the rest of the National Football League. It would be almost a decade before they made it, and one reason it took so long was the way Parker had virtually stripped them of top draft choices for the next three years.

Through all these tribulations, Art Rooney, Sr., added to his reputation for square dealing and philanthropy. Outwardly, he accepted the constant losing with good grace.

In fact, it was Rooney who coined the phrase "Same Old Steelers." The team was showing off new uniforms one day in training camp during those dismal years and Rooney, to be frank, didn't much care for them. "They still look like the same old Steelers to me." he grumbled around his ever present chewed-up cigar, and a Pittsburgh watchword was born.

Still, although he knew something was wrong, Rooney would never interfere with his professional help. He noticed that all the Pittsburgh teams, even the good ones that might have been capable of winning, had one fatal flaw. "It seemed as if they were always sitting there waiting to get beat, waiting for something to happen to them. Why, one year we lost five games in the last two minutes," he said one day as the Steelers were beginning to turn the corner into respectability. The Steelers were like a thoroughbred that always gets beaten in the stretch, no matter how short the race.

As the Steelers began to find success, the white-haired sportsman with the round pink face tried to strip away his "good loser" image.

"I was supposed to be a guy who walked away from defeats

without so much as a second thought, but that's just a lot of nonsense. Every loss in those days got me and I took it right home with me. Losing to me will always be losing. After many years I learned that it doesn't get easier."

Maybe it was just a horse player's fatalism that kept him going. "I'm an old horseman and you learn to be tough in that business," he once said, blinking behind his thick eyeglasses. "Horse racing, you know, is just one disappointment after another."

Yet horsemen also fuel on hope. They know that with the right breeding and the right handicapping, eventually the big score will come. When it did after more than forty years, Art Rooney thoroughly enjoyed it.

9

A Team in Danger

Unfortunately for the poets of football, the Steelers could not end their 1972 season with the Immaculate Reception. Instead, they ran into a team with a destiny of its own, and this time there was a moratorium on miracles.

The week after they beat the Raiders, Pittsburgh met the Miami Dolphins for the American Conference championship. The Dolphins were newcomers to pro football, an expansion team that had not been born until 1966, at which time the Steelers already had been losers for thirty-four seasons. This year the precocious Dolphins had not lost a game and they carried a 15–0 record into Three Rivers Stadium.

All the twists of fate turned against the home team, including the unusual coincidence that by now Terry Bradshaw appeared to have caught Daryle Lamonica's flu. Some time later Chuck Noll would blame reporters for infecting his star players with flu germs, especially out-of-town scribes, presumed carriers of exotic viruses.

The first two touchdowns were perfect examples. The Steelers went ahead, 7–0, when Gerry Mullins recovered a

Bradshaw fumble in the end zone. A good break? Only partially. Bradshaw was hurt on the play and temporarily had to leave the game. Then the Dolphins used a fluke, spontaneous play of their own to set up a tying score when Larry Seiple ran thirty-seven yards on fourth down out of punt formation.

Bob Griese, the Dolphins' regular quarterback, had missed most of the season with a severe ankle injury. He was healthy now, but the Dolphins continued to start the quarterback who had brought them this far, another of those Steeler cast-offs, Earl Morrall. But Morrall and the offense were struggling so in the second half that Miami coach Don Shula went to Griese. Roy Gerela kicked a field goal for a 10–7 Pittsburgh lead, but then Griese directed a pair of touchdown drives to make it 21–10. Bradshaw shook the cobwebs in time to come back for one brilliant scoring drive and a 21–17 score, but that's how it ended. Bradshaw was intercepted twice in the closing minutes as Art Rooney refused to bow to superstition and stayed in his box seat until the final gun. "Maybe I should have gone downstairs again," he grumbled.

Losing to Miami, though, was no disgrace. Everybody who played them did it that year. They completed a perfect 17–0 season by beating Washington, 14–7, in the Super Bowl.

The Steelers would have to wait another year, but now they knew they could play with the best. Noll didn't have to worry about "losing the team." They had come farther than any Steelers in history. It would only be a matter of time. The basis of a team was there.

The development of the Steelers' 1973 draft may have provided additional evidence that a contending cast had been assembled. Art Rooney, Jr.'s personnel department was no less astute, but this time only three players were picked who survived to suit up for the Super Bowl: cornerback Jimmy Thomas, tackle Dave Reavis, and linebacker Loren Toews. "You expect a lot of rookies to make it at first, but if it keeps up year after year it means you're not drafting very well. There should come a time when you need only minimal replacements," Artie explained.

There were two significant retirements Ben McGee, the defensive tackle who had gradually been supplanted by Ernie Holmes, and John Brown, the offensive tackle who had missed all of the 1972 season with knee injuries. Brown, who had played eleven years, still walks with a limp because of an arthritic condition from football, but he insists he would not trade the experience for anything, not even for eternal spring in his legs. He had been very close to the defensive front four, and he would continue to live in Pittsburgh. He'd be there if they needed him.

This, then, was the Steelers' situation in the spring of '73, two days before St. Patrick's Day, when Dan Rooney and Joe Gordon, the publicity director, returned to the office from a meeting. It was after five and the phone was ringing. Mrs. Dan Rooney was calling on her husband's private line.

"Ernie Holmes just called me," she said. "He tried to get you at the office but the switchboard was closed. He's in trouble. You'd better call him right away."

Mrs. Rooney sounded shaken. Dan knew the trouble had to be serious. Just how serious he would discover in a few seconds, when he finished dialing the telephone number she gave him. It was the Mahoning County Jail near Youngstown, Ohio.

When the 1972 season had ended, Fats Holmes should have been a happy man. Financially and football-wise, his stock was rising. But in truth, his world was falling apart. His wife was divorcing him, and when the dissolution was completed she would take with her their two young sons, whom Ernie adored. Ernie's financial affairs also were a mess. He had tried to provide all things to all members of his family. The divorce would be expensive, too. He was over-extended, and there is some question about the kind of schemes in which he may have involved himself to make some money back home in Houston.

Two nights earlier, Ernie had called Dan Rooney in Pitts-burgh. "He was very frightened," Dan recalls. "He needed money and he didn't know how to get it. I think he'd gotten in with a couple of bad characters down there and he said he was really in trouble. He sounded desperate. At first I figured it was just that he needed money to take care of his mother or something, something he was always trying to do even though he was never in that kind of position. But he really seemed to be frightened of the people he was dealing with. He felt alone down there. He said he didn't have any money and he owed more money. I told him, 'Ernie, you don't owe anybody. That will not be a problem. Why don't you come up and see me?'

"We all know there are a lot of pressures in football, but Ernie was able to handle them up here because football is a team thing and he was in a structured situation. But being down there he was alone and it was very frightening."

What Rooney didn't anticipate was that Holmes would immediately jump into his blue and white Cadillac and start driving to Pittsburgh. The distance is over 1,600 miles and Ernie drove straight through without sleep. If there was any chance that he would get through this ordeal without a breakdown, it must have cracked under the strain of this drive. For more than twenty-four hours, Ernie Holmes was alone with his tortured thoughts and fears inside this racing automobile. He was exhausted and yet driven by his obsession. He had to get there, had to find a haven where he could hide from his mounting problems and regroup. He would see Dan Rooney, he would join the Steeler basketball team and pick up a few dollars. Once he did that he would be all right.

It was late the next night when Holmes arrived in Pittsburgh. The Steeler offices, he knew, would be closed. He kept on driving and somehow he found himself on the Pennsylvania Turnpike heading out of Pittsburgh toward Ohio. There was a wreck in one of the tunnels and Holmes was caught in the oppressive jam. Holmes approached a policeman to complain that trucks had been trying to run him off the road. The officer, busy sorting traffic, brushed him off. Back on the highway, he found the truck traffic overwhelming. They would not let him pass, they seemed to be creeping up his tailpipe. On the football field, Ernie Holmes always had an outlet for his frustrations. He'd drive his helmet into somebody's gut and send him staggering back on his heels. He could hit, he could sweat, he could bleed, and when the workout ended a steaming shower would wash it all away. Here he could do nothing but smolder and brood.

Shortly after dawn on Friday he somehow found himself approaching Youngstown, eighty-six miles northwest of Pittsburgh. He was still on the Turnpike. Fatigue, depression, frustration, anger. He reached over and picked up the shotgun he had carried with him. There also was a nine-millimeter automatic pistol in the glove compartment. Guns are part of the Texas life style. Ernie, who grew up on a farm, was a superb marksman. As he sped along, he drew a bead on the tires of a passing truck and fired. He hadn't even bothered to lower his car window. The glass shattered. It was not quite 8 A.M.

As he drove through Youngstown and then circled down and around, he fired at more trucks. By now word was reaching the State Police that some maniac sniper was loose on the highway, shooting at passing trucks—officially four—with a shotgun sticking out his window. The chase was on.

Holmes was spotted and two cars began chasing him at speeds up to ninety miles an hour. He eluded them by pulling off the main highway onto a side road. His left front tire blew, but he sped eleven miles farther on the rim. Finally he spun into a ditch and broke the axle. He grabbed the shotgun and ran off through the fields and into the woods. On the way he lost his sandals.

The State Police spotted his abandoned car and surrounded the area. For five hours Ernie hid undetected in the woods. However, the police had called in a helicopter, and it swooped low over the area. Ernie saw it coming, took his gun, and fired. The pilot was wounded in the ankle as the slugs tore through the floor. Firing at the helicopter proved a mistake in many ways. It gave away his position and some thirty law-enforcement officers closed in. By now it was shortly after two in the afternoon. When Holmes spotted the officers, he pegged a few shots in their direction and they fired back once. Ernie Holmes threw away his gun and surrendered. He addressed the officers as "sir." Said the police: "We could have killed him a dozen times."

Barefoot, wearing an olive-drab tank shirt that exposed

his bulging muscles when his wrists were manacled behind his back, looking confused and distraught, Holmes was led off to jail to be booked for "shooting with intent to kill" at the police officers. After initial hesitation, he called the Steelers.

"How is he?" Dan Rooney asked the policeman who answered the phone at the Mahoning County Jail.

"Pretty bad."

"What happened?"

"He's in a lot of trouble."

Rooney then talked to Holmes. Ernie sounded confused, as if he couldn't fully comprehend what had happened. All he knew was that he was in terrible trouble. He told Rooney he didn't have any shoes.

"We'll do everything we can for you," Rooney promised. "Try not to worry."

Rooney then started to mobilize the Steelers to come to Ernie's rescue. This was not Ernie Holmes. He had never been in trouble before. Some problem, insoluble to him, must have set him off. Dan called the club's attorney, who suggested a lawer in Youngstown. He called Chuck Noll and they made plans to drive to Youngstown the next morning. He called John Brown, who had been very close to Ernie Holmes. In passing, he wondered how Holmes had known his private number at home.

Early reports coming over the radio were sketchy. Art Rooney, Jr., stunned, called information for the phone number of the Mahoning County Jail and asked them to describe this Ernie Holmes. When they got to the gold tooth, his heart fell. It had to be Ernie, the Ernie Holmes of the ready smile, the great way with young kids.

Ed Kiely, director of public relations, got his first tip from a newspaperman as the story was breaking. He immediately called Art Rooney, Sr., in Florida. "But we're not sure it's Ernie; maybe it's just someone using his name," Kiely said hopefully. Rooney hung up to await further word, but he was plenty worried. Always the pragmatist, he wondered why anyone would choose to impersonate Ernie Holmes. If a guy was going to use someone's name, he'd say he was Joe Greene, wouldn't he? Rooney thought to himself. Half an hour later, Kiely called back with the confirmation.

Rooney told Kiely and the others back in Pittsburgh to do what was necessary to help Ernie Holmes. Rooney had once played ball in the Youngstown area and he made some calls to old friends there seeking advice on legal help. "He was our ball player, wasn't he? There was no question about it," Rooney says gruffly when asked about the Steelers' quick commitment. "I think a ball club should do anything it can for one of its people in trouble, unless it's something serious that's going to keep on happening, and then it's an entirely different case. No doubt about it, Ernie was sick."

Were there any warnings before Ernie Holmes went on his rampage? It's hard to tell. Most of his closest friends say not. Dissenting opinions may be tinted by knowledge of the subsequent events. Still, there was the history of problems with his college coach and the way he had abruptly left the Steelers his first season.

"At times Ernie Holmes was a very frightening figure," says a teammate. "Sometimes you did not know what Ernie was thinking and that can make you very uneasy. You weren't sure what his next move was going to be. You got a feeling there was a violence beneath Ernie's surface and if it erupted it could destroy anyone and anything around him. That was an uneasy thing for me and I found other guys had a sense of distance with Ernie, too. You could sense this violent feeling, which did erupt. There is something violent that has to get out and it's a good thing he has football, which is a legitimate avenue, to let it escape."

Says Dwight White: "You know a lot of people tend to laugh at things they may not think are funny because they think they're supposed to. But if Ernie doesn't think it's funny, he doesn't laugh. He's got the kind of personality he can scare you if you don't know him well."

After the ordeal, Holmes, still suspicious, still obsessed with financial matters, worried about making it, still missing his sons painfully, is reluctant to talk about the incident and what brought it on. But this is one case where perhaps the details are less important than the background.

"If you don't have someone to release your problems to, you wind up with a very difficult situation to deal with, one that's kind of heartbreaking at times," he blurted out as we talked, suddenly taking a detour in mid-flight while answering a question about some of the personnel conflicts on the Steelers and how the front four had brought them into the open and resolved them.

"A lot of times even clamming up won't help," he continued. "And I can tell you that myself. I tried to hold it all in and deal with it myself, but if you can't find anyone to ease your system, it forces you to do things that are entirely against your nature."

In conversation, Holmes describes himself as an extremely nonviolent person. He refers to the forces unleashed in his breakdown in the third person, as a separate entity.

"I guess I just overloaded my circuit," he went on. "But now those pressures are off my back and my head is a little clearer. I can sit back now and plan my future and my sons' future. I don't have a different mental approach now, just a more mature idea of things, and I recognize reality a lot better than I did. I'm more mentally sound now. I would hope so. Maybe I'm fooling myself, but I don't think I am."

Dwight White is one who thinks Ernie has survived his ordeal and emerged a stronger person. "I'm just glad to see he came out of this okay and he definitely did get something out of it that was positive," says White. "The thing is, he learned, it wasn't that he just got away with something."

The day after Ernie's arrest, Dan Rooney, Chuck Noll, and John Brown drove to Youngstown. Brown was especially disturbed. Not only was Ernie Holmes his friend, but he knew from personal experience what a terrible ordeal Fats was facing. Before he had decided to go into banking, John Brown had worked in reformatories in the off-season. He knew that if Ernie Holmes had to spend significant time in jail, he might never recover.

"Once you get to that element, you can't get over it," he says. "Maybe a strong man can make it, but a weak man can't, and because of his background he [Holmes] may not be as strong. If you're not strong, you can end up on the corner, and that could be Ernie Holmes if not for football."

Brown tried to convey that insight to Rooney and Noll as they drove to Youngstown. Somehow they had to keep Ernie Holmes out of jail or virtually write him off a as productive member of society.

Still, despite his background, although he knew what to expect, John Brown was shaken at his first glimpse of his friend. "Ernie Holmes, professional football player, in a cell with eight or ten thugs, all of them wearing those brown and gray uniforms."

Holmes was carrying a big stick, like a club. He had heard tales of inmates being molested or beaten up. He told Brown he lay awake on his bunk all night, holding his stick for protection. He catnapped during the day.

Holmes tried to tell Rooney what he remembered about his wild drive, which wasn't much, and they sent out to buy a pair of shoes. All they could find to fit was a pair of basketball sneakers.

It was Saturday and nothing could be done for Holmes over the weekend. "We'll be back Monday," Rooney promised. "Try to make the best of it."

The Monday-morning hearing was held especially early to avoid crowds from traffic court. Holmes was released on $45,000 bond on the Steelers' promise to take him back to Pittsburgh and immediately place him in Western Pennsylvania Psychiatric Hospital. He was expected to be there a month; he remained for two.

During this period, teammates and members of the Pittsburgh family constantly visited with Holmes. Art Rooney, Sr., came by almost every day. L. C. Greenwood took him to town some afternoons. His teammates played cards with him (although never Dwight White, who hates to play cards) and they shot pool in the recreation room. Above all, they cared.

Soon after, Holmes returned to Youngstown and pleaded guilty to charges of assault with a deadly weapon. On June 21, Common Pleas Court Judge Sidney Riegelhaupt, after hearing a Pittsburgh psychiatrist testify that Holmes had been suffering from "acute paranoid psychosis" at the time of the shooting, sentenced him to five years of probation.

"The public good does not demand or require that he be immediately sentenced" to jail, the judge said. He noted that Holmes's character, except for this one incident, was exemplary and that his football earnings would be needed to support his former wife and their two children.

Federal charges of "destruction of interstate property," meaning the trucks, eventually were dropped. The police officer whom Holmes had shot in the ankle later sued Ernie for $700,000, and was awarded $25,000 in a trial just after the Super Bowl. The amount almost exactly equaled Ernie's playoff earnings for the year, but he was happy. "If they'd given that dude what he was asking, they might as well have just put me in the house," he said.

Dan Rooney very dispassionately relates the commitment the Steelers had to make to keep Ernie Holmes from going to jail. He makes it sound so simple. He reluctantly tells how the club paid all of Ernie's bills, bought him a new car, and arranged that he would receive his salary over twelve months rather than in game installments during the season. "Right now he doesn't owe anybody but us," Rooney says. The team also promised to see to it that Ernie continued to receive psychiatric help after he left the hospital and to try to get him a job when he was up to it. As part of his probation, Ernie was to make his home in Pittsburgh, close to his new support.

"The judge was able to see that the only thing that could save Ernie was football," Rooney says.

The Steelers' commitment, of course, went far beyond this. They were putting themselves squarely on the line with their unequivocal support of a man who, after all, had been shooting at people—and had hit one of them. They trusted their gut feeling that Ernie Holmes was a good man who had suffered what Dwight White calls "a bump in the road." This black kid from rural Texas who had found himself in a world he couldn't completely understand or cope with deserved the same kind of second chance as rich whites who could afford their own psychiatrists to treat them and testify for them. Since the Steelers are in the public image business, it was a real risk.

"A lot of people in football are afraid they're going to be contaminated by public opinion when something like that happens," says Chuck Noll, one of many who felt "It must be another Ernie Holmes" when he first heard the news.

"The thing that I appreciate about the Rooneys is that they are not concerned about their 'reputations,' they are concerned about helping a guy and doing everything they can for someone in trouble."

When he visited Holmes in jail, Noll says, "I realized he needed professional help. . . . The things is, football provides an outlet for Ernie and Ernie can make a contribution to society through football. Ernie is an extremely fine person and I didn't want to see him wreck his life."

John Brown reacts emotionally when he talks about what the Steelers did for Ernie Holmes. "They could have let him rot," Brown says softly but with feeling as he sits massively behind his desk in the branch office of a Pittsburgh bank. "Sure he was a good ball player, but there are fifty million ball players and at that point he wasn't even that important a ball player. Heck, they had put him on waivers the year before.

"They could have let him drown, and they didn't," Brown

continues. "Here's a little black boy and they could have let him drown. But they cared; they went beyond caring, because to all intents and purposes, Ernie Holmes could be in jail right now.

"Today, though, he is somebody. He is Ernie Holmes of the World Champion Pittsburgh Steelers. That may be more important to Ernie in terms of getting him situated in society than anything. Joe is strong and Joe is already Joe Greene. L. C. has his own thing, he is Hollywood Bags, he has his own mystique. Dwight is a pretty smart young man and he is stable. Ernie is not as stable as these other fellows and the thing now is for him to get himself together in terms of his future."

Holmes himself is unashamedly grateful to the Steelers. "If you could add someone to your family, I would add Art Rooney," he says. He discloses that he turned down a $65,000 bonus from the World Football League to jump leagues, and when he crossed the picket line to report to camp during the next summer's players' strike, he asked, "Wouldn't you be loyal to the man who saved your life?"

The events behind Ernie's crossing the line tell something about how the Steelers operate. They kept communications open with their strikers as all concerned feared a bitter rupture might damage the team's chances once the dispute was settled. Dan Rooney made it clear to the strike leaders that he wasn't trying to break their strike through this tactic, but that it would be in Ernie's best interest to be in camp. He needed the controlled atmosphere. Ernie admits it. "I guess I'm a military type individual and football is like a military drill. You enlist in high school and go on up through the ranks." The players agreed. They made it easy for Ernie

Holmes to show his gratitude to the Rooneys by reporting to camp. Dan Rooney insists that this is a gesture the Steelers never felt he "owed" them.

Winning the Super Bowl was a great achievement, but to many people, the Pittsburgh Steelers' finest moment came when Ernie Holmes trotted out on the field to open the 1973 football season. Because of their support, Ernie Holmes had returned to society.

While Ernie Holmes was undergoing his rehabilitation, the Steelers were not completely idle. They did not know if he would have to go to jail and, even if he was physically available to play, what would be the state of his mental health? Could he hold up through a season?

To protect themselves, they traded a third-round draft choice to Oakland for Tom Keating, a bright, intelligent defensive tackle who had been a major star in the early days of the American Football League. By now, however, he was approaching his thirty-first birthday and he had never recovered his old quickness after undergoing surgery for a torn Achilles tendon that had kept him out of action for an entire season in 1968.

The Steelers were quite pragmatic about the deal. "We were concerned whether Ernie would be there to play football," Chuck Noll explains frankly. "There was a good chance he was going to end up in jail, and even if he didn't we were concerned about how he would function. We had some young ones we felt would come along, but we also felt we were ready to make a push and go for the championship, and we needed someone with experience. Keating was available and so we traded for him."

Holmes was crushed when he heard about the deal. He

would not accept the Steelers' explanation that they felt they needed to protect themselves in case his recovery was not complete.

"I knew why they brought him in, it was as a threat to me, to apply pressure, to test my ability," he insists to this day. "They thought I would relax with no pressure behind me. But if you're considered a pro, you don't need any pressure."

So, for the second straight year, Ernie Holmes was faced with the prospect of sharing duty at right tackle.

Keating, for his part, was awed by his new teammates. He's white and so friends described him as "the lump of sugar in the coal bin." He told teammates, "You know, I'm a defensive tackle too, but I'm afraid of these guys." Then he'd rush off to the weight room to try to build more muscles.

Whatever the stimulus, whether it was Keating's presence or just the year's experience, Ernie Holmes played superbly in 1973. As had happened the season before with McGee, pretty soon he was playing most of the time. Keating eventually saw only spot duty, except when Holmes was hurt. When the Steelers routed Cleveland, 33–6, for their second straight victory, Ernie Holmes had five solo tackles, eight assists, and three quarterback sacks. He was awarded the game ball and Noll pointed out that the Browns had paid him an even greater tribute. "They double teamed him," Noll said. "It's the first time that's happened." Normally this double attention was reserved for Joe Greene alone.

The Steelers started out with four straight victories, lost in Cincinnati, then won four more for an 8–1 record. They were riding high toward the playoffs.

However, in game seven, a victory over the Bengals, Terry

Bradshaw suffered a shoulder separation. He would be out for months. The next week, Terry Hanratty suffered cracked ribs.

The Steelers were able to patch up Hanratty for the next week's game in Oakland, where this now bitter rivalry was renewed with even greater feeling. Dwight White led the way for the front four in this game. He had two interceptions, three sacks, and nine tackles, and was named AP Defensive Player of the Week for his role in the 17–9 triumph. But even though they won, the Steelers left the field muttering obscenities. Joe Greene claimed Oakland guard George Buehler and others had greased their jerseys to make it tougher for the defensive linemen to use their hands to fling them aside. The Steelers claimed the Raiders ran in a mushy underinflated football on them when it was time to punt.

Although the charges were never proved in a league investigation, Greene to this day insists, "Buehler had grease on his jersey." Noll and many of the Steelers who were new to the machinations of Oakland and its managing general partner, Al Davis, were enraged and upset by these supposed tactics, which was the general idea. Some of the old AFL guys like John Dockery were amused. They'd been putting up with these Oakland ploys for years. "So the ball is flat, you bring your own pump. What else is new out here?" Dockery laughed.

There was little to laugh about the next three weeks, however. The following Sunday, the Steelers lost to Denver, 23–13, their first defeat at home in two years. Hanratty had been playing all the while despite excrutiating pain from his ribs, but the next week he hurt his wrist in the first quarter and had to be relieved by young Joe Gilliam in a 21–16 loss to

Cleveland. Cleveland's winning touchdown was set up by a Gilliam fumble.

Gilliam got his first start the next Monday night in Miami and the Dolphins opened up a 27–0 lead as Joe Gilly was intercepted three times. By now Bradshaw was getting well, and so he replaced the shaken youngster to spark a ferocious Pittsburgh rally. Near the end Miami had to resort to a play hardly ever seen in the pros. Backed to their goal line on fourth down, the Dolphins took a deliberate safety so they could get off a free kick without any danger that it would be blocked. Larry Seiple boomed one seventy yards and the Dolphins held on for a 30–26 victory.

The defeat was the Steelers' third straight, and dropped them into a three-way tie for the division lead with Cleveland and Cincinnati. However, the Steelers closed with victories over Houston and San Francisco for a 10–4 record. Cincinnati had the same record, but under the NFL's tie-breaking procedures, the Bengals were declared division winners. Pittsburgh would make the playoffs as the wild card team.

Once again the Steelers drew Oakland in the first round, but this time they would have to play the Raiders out on the Coast. Once again there were pregame incidents. Nobody's head got bashed, but ugly words were exchanged.

The final weekend of the regular season, the Steelers were scheduled in San Francisco on Saturday while the Raiders were at home to Denver the next afternoon in a game that would decide the Western Division championship and along with it Pittsburgh's first-round opponent. The Steelers planned to spend the week in Palm Springs, California, to await the first round of the playoffs, and they headed there immediately after their game.

Noll, however, thought it would be a good idea to leave several coaches behind to scout Oakland-Denver. NFL rules require that teams must provide one press-box scouting ticket to any of its opponents who ask, but on this occasion the Steelers requested three. Since they didn't know which team they would be playing, the Steelers felt this was justified because they would have to scout both sides until the issue was decided. The Raiders turned them down. The Steelers offered to buy the extra tickets in the stands. The Raiders turned them down. The Steelers appealed to the commissioner. The commissioner turned them down.

At this point, publicity director Joe Gordon had an idea. Knowing the Steelers had planned to stay out West, he had ordered press-box credentials for several writers in case they wanted to cover this game. All, however, preferred to remain in Palm Springs so they could be close to the team and the sunshine. Gordon suggested to Dan Rooney that their assistant coaches use these tickets.

The coaches had no difficulty entering the stadium, but they made the mistake of going out on the field before the game. They were spotted and hustled off the grass. Thus tipped off, the Raiders had police officers and a club official waiting at the press-box entrance. The Steeler coaches were barred, but if they wanted to remain in the stadium and watch the action as standees, that would be fine. George Perles was one of the coaches. In frustration, he told diminutive Al LoCasale of the Raider front office, "You're too small to hit. I think I'll slap you to death."

The Steelers were embarrassed and reprimanded for their attempted subterfuge, but this was nothing compared to the way they must have felt the next weekend. Ernie Holmes was hurt and so Tom Keating drew the start against his old teammates, who ran right at him from the beginning and blew him out of the ball park. But Keating couldn't be blamed for the loss. A lot of people had to play poorly for Oakland to roll up 361 yards in total offense in a 33–14 rout. No miracles could help the Steelers make up the difference, and Chuck Noll summed up the game in one simple declarative sentence: "They beat the hell out of us."

There were several reasons for Pittsburgh's late collapse. One, of course, was the series of injuries to both top quarterbacks, Bradshaw and Hanratty, plus Gilliam's obvious unreadiness to step in. Also, Franco Harris had a disappointing year. He, too, was bothered by a series of nagging and somewhat mysterious injuries. He did not start until the sixth game of the season and in two of these he did not play at all. Although he led the team in ground gaining for the second straight year, his yardage dropped from 1,055 to 698.

Joe Greene had an ordinary year, too; not bad for most players, but quite uninspired for a player of his stature. He tried not to use his back problems as an excuse, but even though Ernie Holmes played quite well, the Steeler defense without inspirational play from its leader was not overpowering. Six teams gave up fewer points than Pittsburgh.

But there were disturbing intangibles, too. Dwight White, looking back, says, "We felt after our good start we could coast to the division title. When we lost those three games in a row our bubble burst and we never recovered." Both of the Steelers' two closing victories had come against weak teams, 1–13 Houston and 5–9 Frisco.

One Steeler began to doubt whether the team as currently constituted could make it all the way. "Oakland just ran us off the field," he said. "Their offensive line handled our defensive line, and I began to wonder whether I would have to reappraise our talent. Who was going to lead the offense? Terry Bradshaw? Terry Hanratty was the favorite of a lot of fellows on the team. Can you lean totally on your defense? And if the defense is that good, who is going to lead it? Joe Greene? Could Joe Greene do it week in and week out? In the past he had not. The potential to play bad football was there."

Joe Greene seemed to be thinking much the same way when he reported to camp the next summer.

Talking to *Pittsburgh Post-Gazette* Sports Editor Bill Christine, Greene admitted, "We are a team in danger. We are in danger of living on potential and no one can do that. You are powerless with potential. I fear the Steelers might become like teams I remember from the past, like the Cardinals in the days when they were always expected to win in their division, but never did.

"I don't think you could point to any one game that makes or breaks a season, but I felt that if we were to regain our pride, something I think we lost, it should have come after the Miami game. The Dolphins had us down twenty-seven points at the half and we came back and only lost by four. I thought it would put us on the way back, but it didn't work out that way."

The Steelers had just completed the two greatest seasons in their history. They had made the playoffs for the second straight year. But still they were dissatisfied; they were questing and questioning. Maybe this was a good sign. Their goals were set higher.

10

The Odd 4-3

For a man of Chuck Noll's orderly mind, the opening of the 1974 season had to be a nightmare. Coaches spend several weeks in the spring mapping plans for training camp, which generally opens in early July. Daily workout programs are scheduled to the minute and any NFL coach can tell you in June what he will be doing at 10 A.M. on August 3—and with whom.

On July 1, 1974, however, three days before the first rookies were to report to camp, the NFL Players Association called a strike. Those meticulous schedules were suddenly rendered obsolete. The players presented a list of more than ninety demands, and the owners vowed to resist no matter what the cost. They persuaded their rookies to cross the picket lines and signed dozens of free agents almost literally off the streets to flesh out their rosters. They played exhibition games with virtual pickup teams and paid refunds to those fans who demanded them. At a loss of $12 million (their figure), the owners brought the union to its knees. In mid-August, faced with mounting defections, the association agreed to return to work and go through the season without a contract.

The Steelers found themselves opening training camp without an established quarterback. In desperation, they traded a rookie running back named Doug Kotar to the Giants for a quarterback who at least had been to a couple of pro camps, Leo Gasienica. When Kotar proved outstanding in several Giants preseason games and actually made the team, the Steelers had the grace to look embarrassed.

There were other strike-related quarterback developments, however, that affected the team even more deeply and eventually would put the front four squarely in the middle of what could have been a team-shattering crisis.

On July 29, the Monday before Pittsburgh's first preseason game, Joe Gilliam, the young black quarterback coming back for his third try, crossed the picket line and reported to camp. Eight days later, Terry Bradshaw defected from the union. And eight days after that, when the union leadership called its strike moratorium, Terry Hanratty reported with the last of the veterans. For several years, Noll had been able to maintain an uneasy balance between his two Terrys at quarterback. Bradshaw was number one, but Hanratty got playing time and actually had played a major role during the 1973 season. The strike destroyed this balance.

What happened was that Gilliam started the first exhibition game as the only experienced quarterback on the grounds. Bradshaw was ready soon afterward, but following game three he developed an inflamed tendon in his right forearm. It was the equivalent of a baseball pitcher's sore arm and he got it the same way most pitchers do, by trying to throw too hard too soon. Bradshaw missed game four, and although he played well in the last two exhibitions, Gilliam by this time was performing brilliantly. The Steelers went undefeated in six games, their best recorded preseason log in history.

As the opener approached, even Bradshaw had to admit, "Gilliam deserves to start."

Hanratty ended up third in a three-man race. By holding out, he may have strengthened his already warm rapport with the other veterans, but he lost whatever chance he had to win the starting job. Gilliam, on the other hand, was a major beneficiary of the strike. Those close to the Steelers say there was no way he would have beaten Bradshaw out if they had started at the same time.

Now we must flash back to Bradshaw's rookie season. When he arrived in 1970, the Steelers disposed of Dick Shiner, but Hanratty remained. Bradshaw's arrival was universally hailed in Pittsburgh. Steeler fans thought he would do for their team what they thought Joe Namath had done for the Jets. The years had conveniently fogged their memories. Joe Namath had not turned the Jets into instant winners anywhere but at the box office. They did not win a championship of any kind or go to the Super Bowl until his fourth season. However, Steeler fans preferred to think that Joe Willie had been an instant success, and they expected Bradshaw to live up to this false memory.

The funny thing is that he did it . . . in preseason. The Steelers lost their first exhibition game, then swept the next four. Bradshaw was outstanding. He couldn't be blamed for figuring this must be a pretty easy game.

However, when he and the team fell back to their own level for a 5–9 record, Bradshaw came apart emotionally.

He found himself unable to cope with the disappointment. When benched in favor of Hanratty, he pouted and hinted he wanted to be traded. He just wasn't ready.

The Steelers, of course, weren't about to give up on Bradshaw, no matter how much he thought about giving up on himself. Each subsequent season he was reinstated as number one quarterback, with Hanratty available to come out of the bullpen.

As the years went on, however, the "book" on Bradshaw became common knowledge in football. He simply was not that quick in a football sense. Hanratty had a much better command of the offense and a better ability to improvise when things went wrong. What he didn't have was Bradshaw's arm and Noll's confidence. Bradshaw also showed a disconcerting tendency to rattle under pressure. The quarterback is supposed to be the rock of a football team. He must keep his head when all about him are losing theirs. Stories were told of situations where Bradshaw would be struck dumb in the huddle and one of the wide receivers would have to call the play to avoid a wasted time out or a penalty for delay of game. Some of Bradshaw's play-calling in big games defied explanation, although Noll steadfastly refused to follow the expedient of calling all plays from the bench. He'd seen enough of that when he was playing for the Browns.

Into this scene in 1972 strolled Joe Gilliam, brash and bright son of a Tennessee State assistant coach. Gilliam idolized Broadway Joe Namath and often referred to himself as Joe Willie Gilly or Jefferson Street Joe, after Nashville's main drag.

He was a picture quarterback prospect, although a little skinny at 6'2", 187 pounds, and showed impeccable college credentials. The NFL has a hard time denying its subconscious prejudice against black quarterbacks when the record shows that Joe Gilliam was not drafted until the eleventh round. A total of 272 players were chosen ahead of him, including such quarterback forgettables as Van Brownson of Nebraska, Dean Carlson of Iowa State, Craig Curry of Minnesota, and Mike Frank of East New Mexico State, and such highly touted busts (at least till now) as Pat Sullivan of Auburn, Jerry Tagge of Nebraska, and John Reaves of Florida.

Gilliam, whose arm may be even stronger than Bradshaw's for sheer velocity, was aware that NFL teams in the past had taken versatile black quarterbacks and shunted them off to other positions that did not require leadership. When he reported to his first Steeler camp, he deliberately ran the forty at less than full speed. Too many black quarterbacks in the past had run themselves right into the defensive secondary the first day. He was a quarterback and a quarterback he would be.

For two years Gilliam's presence created few problems. He was raw and inexperienced and he came from a small college background. (As did Bradshaw.) He needed time. Although he chafed on the taxi squad, realistically he could not complain about his treatment. There were two other young quarterbacks ahead of him. In 1973, his second season, when the two Terrys were hurt, Gilliam showed emphatically that he was not ready for the pressure of being number one.

However, 1974 was different. Gilliam was ready to play, and no matter what the extenuating circumstances of strike and injury may have been, he flat out won the job in training camp.

In the season opener, he passed for 257 yards in a 30–0

victory over Baltimore. The next week he attempted fifty passes and completed thirty-one of them for 357 yards in a 35–35 overtime tie with Denver. In two games, Joe Willie Gilly, crediting tips he had gotten from Joe Namath while serving as an instructor in the master's summer football camp, had put sixty-five points in the board. Once again Bradshaw was mumbling about wanting to be traded. It was turning into a bad year for Terry. He hurt his arm and lost his starting job, and his wife divorced him.

The next week, however, the honeymoon ended for Gilliam, too. The Steelers were shut out at home by hated Oakland, 17–0, and the fans brutally turned on the young quarterback. Where once they had reviled Bradshaw, now they cheered as blond Terry began to warm up in the final quarter. The fans overlooked the fact that Pittsburgh's best running back, Franco Harris, had gone down with a sprained ankle on the first play of the game. They wanted Gilliam's head. Eventually they got it.

Noll cannot be accused of abandoning Gilliam. He kept him at the helm for three more games, but he was not the Joe Gilly of old. He forgot that there were running plays in the offense. As if in desperation to show what he could do, he seemed to be passing on every down. The Steelers won those next three games, but not by much. They barely beat Houston, 13–7; they needed a hatful of interceptions to stop Kansas City, 34–24, although Gilliam did have a good day against this fading team; and then they required a saving interception and Roy Gerela's field goals to beat Cleveland, 20–16, as Gilliam went 5-for-18.

After six games of the season, even though his team still showed a 4–1–1 record with three straight victories, Noll benched Gilliam in favor of Bradshaw. This was a daring move, but Bradshaw didn't seem to be the answer, either. The Steelers won two more for a streak of five, but then lost to Cincinnati, and Noll made another change. He dumped Bradshaw and announced that Hanratty would start the following week in Cleveland, where Pittsburgh had not won a game in ten years. The Steelers won, 26–16, but it was Joe Greene who made the big scoring play. With the score tied at 16-all in the fourth quarter, he recovered a fumble and then lateraled off to cornerback J. T. Thomas, who ran fourteen yards for the winning touchdown. Hanratty's performance was abysmal. He threw fifteen passes and only five were caught—three of them by the other team. Gilliam finished up with 1-for-4, which isn't even very good for baseball.

As could be expected, Noll was bombarded with criticism. For the first and perhaps only time in his career, he threw up his hands. What could he do? he asked. He didn't like all this shuffling, either. He pointed out that the quarterbacks were partly to blame, too. "I just wish one of them would take the bull by the horns and win the job," he complained.

The next week Bradshaw was reinstated as number one quarterback.

Quarterback conflict is always unsettling to a football team. Players can't help but take sides. Whether it's based on friendship or dispassionate evaluation, each player has his own idea as to who would do the best job. Such situations have destroyed ball clubs. In Pittsburgh, there were two added dimensions. Three, not two quarterbacks were involved—and one of them was black.

Since about half the Steeler squad is composed of black players, there could easily have been a squad revolt, especially since Gilliam was benched with a winning record. Nobody realizes this more than Noll, although he will not publicly discuss this aspect. He will not disagree, however, when it is mentioned, nor will he argue that it was the all-black front four, the most influential and cohesive unit on the team, that prevented any thoughts of a revolt from surfacing. No matter what their personal feelings, they outwardly took the quarterback shuffle in stride and refused to let it deter them from their primary goal, getting to the Super Bowl.

Joe Greene, from the confidence of his position, talks about the situation most freely.

"Sure the quarterback situation hurt our team," he says. "For a while we were struggling. Mainly it hurt our receivers. They didn't know from one week to the next who the hell would be throwing the ball. It hurt our timing and made us look unorganized at times. But we're a good football team, and good football teams can withstand that kind of situation. I don't think it's the best situation, but we did what we had to do. We got behind the guy who was quarterbacking at the time. That's the way I looked at it, and I'm sure that's the way the other guys went at it. I never got any angry vibes from the other guys.

"We never really got into any heavy conversation about the idea of a black quarterback. I pulled for Joe in the sense of what he'd mean for other black kids. They'd say, 'Hey, Joe is doing it and Harris [James Harris of the Rams] is doing it and so maybe there's a chance I can play quarterback in the NFL.'

"But as far as the team was concerned, it was purely selfish on my part. All I wanted was for the best guy to play. I pulled for Bradshaw, I pulled for Hanratty, and I pulled for Joe. I was rooting for the guy who could bring us, whichever one was in there."

Greene's protective streak extends beyond his colleagues on the front four. He resents boos and jeers, no matter where they're aimed, and he knew Terry Bradshaw had taken more than his share longer than the others.

"Nobody pulled more for Bradshaw than I did," he continued. "I was pulling harder for him than he or his parents were. I was always opposed to the way Pittsburgh [fans] treated Terry. They gave him a raw deal. He came in as the number one draft choice, the number one pick in the country, the savior, and it didn't happen right away. And when Terry didn't do it, they slapped back at him. They gave him a bum deal and I'm damn glad he gave them the last laugh."

Greene is aware of the racial vibrations in blue-collar Pittsburgh. He thought it offensive when some writers tried to pin the tag of the Black Jacks on the Steeler front four. He noted racial overtones in the fans' reaction to Gilliam.

"We opened the season against Baltimore," he recalls. "Joe wanted the job, no doubt about it, and he should have been starting, and Chuck started him. Well, he threw his first pass and when it went up in the air the fans were booing and when it came down they were cheering. Right then I knew it was a black-white thing.

After he began to have some success in preseason games, Gilliam went to the media and told them that he preferred that his name be pronounced Gill-um. The change jarred Pittsburgh radio listeners and there was some reaction. Pittsburgh fans react to everything. Those who called in were about evenly divided. Half thought the announcers were making fun of Joe now that he was somebody, and the other half accused him of becoming "uppity" now that he was doing well.

Greene has long been in Chuck Noll's corner. He likes and respects the man. Noll is not a screamer. The other members of the front four appreciate this. They also appreciate his football knowledge, and if he is cold-blooded, at least that eliminates any possibility of racial prejudice. Green goes along with the decision to settle on Bradshaw. "Quarterback wasn't the reason we were losing," Greene says, "but Noll just decided to put Bradshaw in and let him grow with us."

Greene reacts just as angrily to blacks who may still criticize Noll for benching Gilliam. "What do they want, blood?" he exclaims. "We won the Super Bowl [with Bradshaw], give the man his due. What he did wasn't a slap at Joe. Heck, Joe played six games this year and before that he played two. That's not a whole lot of experience under fire. Joe's going to get better."

Dwight White doesn't underplay the dangers of the quarterback situation.

"If we didn't have the mental maturity that everybody had to have, from the coaches down, it could have been enough to destroy the whole team," White says. "There was a lot of dissension among the fans. They fluctuated constantly, although there was no real logic to their complaints that I could see. But a situation like that definitely could have wiped us out, certainly as the season began to drag on, because when you've been so close to a bunch of guys for so many days, day in and day out, you naturally begin to get itchy and irritable.

"I didn't personally get off into the quarterback thing," White continues. "I was just interested in winning, and the quarterback who was the hottest was the quarterback I wanted to go with. I didn't care. They're all good quarterbacks and I would hate to play against any of them. The thing is as long as we win, and if we could win without a quarterback, that would be okay, too. I don't have time to figure out who's the best quarterback because it's not relevant to what I do. I've got to play defensive end.

"As for Joe Gilly, I can't say I was pulling for him more, because in competition, the best man will always win."

Of course, not all Steelers are as self-motivated as Dwight White and as able to compartmentalize their lives, because on a broader canvas, White certainly is able to feel deeply the wounds of racism. Racial undercurrents did exist on the team, especially with the emergence of Joe Gilliam. Terry Bradshaw is very blond, very white, and very southern, at least in speech and appearance, although whatever attitudes he may have grown up with were obviously left behind in Shreveport. What kept the Steelers on track was the obvious absence of any prejudice in Steeler management, including the coaching staff. The Rooneys' support of Ernie Holmes erased any possible accusation of hypocrisy, and nobody knew this better than the front four.

The strike and the quarterback situation weren't the only unsettling elements as the Steelers headed into the 1974 campaign. There was also the threat of the World Football League. Would his future contract affect L. C. Greenwood's lame-duck season? Some WFL jumpers had been active recruiters for the new league. On the other side, some NFL teams had been treating their lame ducks as if they had broken sacred vows rather than followed standard business procedure to improve their fortunes. Good players were vindictively cut or traded off to unattractive teams during the summer.

Noll predictably played it cool. If he mentioned the WFL at all, it was to the effect that "we know it's here and we know some guys are thinking of leaving, but that is next year and we are concerned with this season."

Privately, though, he admits he was watching L. C. Greenwood's performance more closely than usual. They never discussed the situation, but Noll adds dryly, "If he hadn't produced the way he did, I probably would have had a talk with him. But he had his best year."

Greenwood obviously was uncomfortable as he reported to camp. He knew the others would be watching him. He didn't know what kind of reaction to expect from teammates, coaches, or management. Neither, of course, did the Steelers. Would L. C. take a pass? "I think you could say we feared that kind of situation," Dan Rooney admits. "I think that was the first thing everybody thought of whenever a player signed with the WFL. But the more I thought about it, the more I realized that L. C. was the kind of guy who was not going to let his performance slip. If there was a player who would not let the lame-duck situation bother him, L. C. was it."

Dan Rooney made certain to reassure Greenwood about his place in the Steeler family. He was still a member of the team until he actually changed jerseys.

His teammates, however, were not so kind. Locker-room humor can be raw and merciless, as well as generally profane. Even Ernie Holmes occasionally would be reminded of his recent troubles, especially if a helicopter appeared where the Steelers might be working out. Greenwood was given the treatment. Hollywood was forgotten, and for now he was Birmingham Bags.

L. C. kidded back. "In Birmingham, I bet I get better shoes than you got here, and I'll have a bigger car and a penthouse apratment," he'd boast, but he also seriously defended his position as one made strictly on financial grounds and to protect his best interests. The players respected his forthright stand—many jumpers kept their future signings secret—and they recognized quickly that he was working harder than ever in training camp.

Only one other Steeler would sign a future WFL contract. Frenchy Fuqua signed with the New York Stars, but for delivery several seasons hence, after his multiyear Pittsburgh contract was up. By that time he would be over thirty. Fuqua missed most of the season with wrist and hand injuries that required surgery, and it was his absence that eventually led the Steelers to settle on Viet Nam war hero Rocky Bleier as the perfect halfback complement to Franco Harris. Babe Parilli, fired earlier as Steeler quarterback tutor, was head coach of the Stars. He tried to get both Bradshaw and Hanratty to jump, but both elected to remain with Pittsburgh. These were the Steelers most celebrated WFL cases.

During the early weeks of the season, the Steelers received still another start. One day after the first Houston game, Ernie Holmes showed up with his head shaved bald. This was not unusual. He had done this before. "I'm a young man and I'm losing my hair," he explains. "This is the best way to hide my baldness, and besides, it doesn't fall out so fast."

A week later, however, Ernie's hair was growing back, but shaped in the unmistakable form of an arrowhead.

Oh, no, thought Art Rooney, Jr. The guy's in trouble again.

Ernie Holmes had not however, flipped his wig, so to speak. Although there obviously were deep psychological reasons underlying this hunger for recognition, the arrow-head haircut in actuality was a calculated ploy by Ernie Holmes to get some publicity.

For the last three years he had been the fourth and least recognized member of the defensive line. Many thought he had played even better than Joe Greene in 1973, Ernie's first as a full-time regular, yet it was Joe Greene who got the big salary, made the all-star teams, was tapped for commercial endorsements. Ernie Holmes was the only member of the front four who had never been invited to play in the Pro Bowl.

This season marked the first time in his career that he had no competition for the starting job. He was accepted as number one at his position, and for a while what he called "one of the greatest things that ever happened to me" was satisfaction enough. But still public recognition seemed to elude him.

Ever since his first season, Fats had been searching for some method of drawing attention to himself. He says he figured some sort of zany hairstyle might be the thing, but then came his troubles with the law, and the subsequent season was a good time to maintain a low profile.

As the 1974 campaign approached, however, Ernie Holmes again was pondering ways to become famous, to grab the headlines and endorsements that would make him rich with residuals.

Before the first Houston game down there, to use his words,

"I balded my head." His mother was at the game. He says she not only liked it but "she gave me incentive to make more of it," which may be the most incredible part of the whole story.

Anyway, as in the cartoons where an electric light suddenly turns on to indicate "Idea!" Ernie Holmes says he got the inspiration for the arrowhead design one morning the next week while half asleep. He sprang out of bed, rushed down to the stadium, and began shaving the design into the fuzz that had just started to grow back after the previous week's balding.

Except for a later game in New Orleans when he was ill and knew he couldn't play, he carefully trimmed and shaped his arrow every week. It was a task he would not entrust to any barber, so personal had the design come to be. Thus Fats Holmes became known as Arrowhead, at least once in a while.

The arrow is more than a haircut to Ernie Holmes; quite a bit more.

"It represents a great deal to me as an individual and it represents my philosophy of life," he says. "If an individual is going to stand up and be recognized, he must stand up in front of the sun and cast a shadow. But if there's two or three individuals standing in the sunlight and casting shadows, each of these shadows is going to be focused in a different direction. I'm an individual who has a dream, a desire to go forward.

"The arrow to me also represents tranquility and peace of mind, and it's a thing of individual pride. It's not something that anybody put on me or that I have to share with anyone. I did it all myself.

"That stuff about the arrow pointing the way to the quarterback is just a line some people threw in—although when I get to the quarterback, I do like to attack with the head. I get my kicks out of that."

Weird, bizarre, but effective. The arrow and Ernie Holmes became famous. He still didn't make the Pro Bowl, but he did get recognition on some all-star teams and whenever he got in range of a camera, the helmet came off and the arrow was recorded.

"Maybe it will be nice to retire it after the Super Bowl," he suggested with his gold tooth shining out of a sly-as-a-fox grin. But some arrow-related endorsements were reported in the works and the retirement figured to be short-lived.

The Steelers' quarterback dilemma did not end with Noll's decision to reinstate Bradshaw. Within a week the grandstand coaches were busy again. With Steve Furness playing well in place of the ailing Holmes, Bradshaw directed Pittsburgh to a 28–7 victory over New Orleans. But the next Sunday, as a freezing rain soaked Three Rivers Stadium, the Steelers were upset by Houston, 13–10. The ineffective Bradshaw had to leave the game with bruised ribs and Hanratty replaced him.

The first question Noll was asked after this disappointing loss concerned his quarterback. What now? Would he make still another change only two weeks before the end of the season with the division championship and playoff berth still not assured? Noll said he would not. Bradshaw was still his quarterback. The rib injury was not deemed serious.

The loss was a shocking one to the Steelers. Although the Oilers had been playing well lately, they were still a team the

Steelers should have beaten. Instead, Houston dominated the game.

"We had expected them to lay down to the sword carriers, which they didn't; they came with swords themselves and took them to us" is the way Ernie Holmes describes the defeat.

The year before, the Steelers had cruised through the initial games in their schedule in high gear, only to fall apart at the first adversity. Thanks to their good start, they made the playoffs, but had nothing left. This time, however, they knew how to cope with defeat. Instead of getting down, they rededicated themselves. In the end, they would call the Houston loss the turning point of their season, their springboard into the Super Bowl.

There were meetings the next Tuesday when the players reported again for practice. According to Holmes, Chuck Noll "asked us all to search our souls and come out with a logical reason why we lost."

There was a players-only meeting as well, ostensibly devoted to matters dealing with their union. Many of the veterans spoke about the need to get themselves together for the final push. Joe Greene reportedly had a lot to say, but he denies it. "Maybe they just could tell what I was thinking," he says of these reports.

Later Noll would call the Houston loss "probably our low point." He points out that "we didn't play well at all, but we came back the next week and said to ourselves, We better cut out all this nonsense and get after this thing. We've got it in our grasp, it's there for the taking, and we're not going to blow it."

George Perles, so close to his front four, vividly recalls the situation.

"We lost confidence, we were scared, we were insecure," he says. "It was a real flustrating loss, especially for us up front, and we went into our meetings the next week in hopes of correcting our mistakes and searching our souls. It was a real turning point in our season because we lost confidence and we didn't have any answers."

Perles took some of the blame for that loss on behalf of the coaching staff. "They ran on us inside because we had anticipated them going wide. It was one of the few times we ever got caught playing defense that particular way."

From that point on, however, the Steelers would stake everything on a new defense Perles had devised and which they had used only sparingly up to that point. They would unveil it full-time the next week against New England, and after this game Patriot center Bill Lenkaitis would complain, "It was the most miserable spot I've ever been in."

The source of Bill Lenkaitis's misery was known as the "Odd 4–3," and it would become nationally famous as the tactic of Pittsburgh's defensive dominance in the Super Bowl. The inventor was George Perles, although he insists he had four eager collaborators who helped him implement the scheme.

"Nobody ever wrote it down and said, 'This is the way it's going to be done,'" Perles says in describing the evolution of the alignment that would prove so effective in the playoffs.

In pro ball, there are two basic defensive line fronts, odd and even. In an odd defense, there is a defender head-on opposite the center. Many teams in 1974 used an odd defense with only three linemen and four linebackers. It was successful early, but near the end of the year the offense figured out how to beat it. In an even defense, the standard pro 4–3, the center is left uncovered with the defensive tackles opposite the guards.

Pittsburgh's Odd 4–3 combined the best features of both. Ernie Holmes and Joe Greene, the tackles, both lined up in a position to menace the center, which accounts for the discomfort of Bill Lenkaitis and his friends. To make it more awesome, Greene eventually suggested that he line up at an angle with his body half turned toward the center. It certainly had an intimidating effect, but the main purpose was to present less of a blocking surface to the guards. Later Holmes suggested that he might line up a little off the ball to be in position to stunt or loop behind the swifter-charging Greene. (The defense also was known occasionally as the Stunt 4–3.) The offense faced the terrible problem of never knowing which of the tackles would bowl over the center and which guard spot would take the brunt of the other tackle's charge. Or if the center would be ignored and both guards attacked.

Here's how Perles explains it:

"Normally, when you have a man on the center, the guards aren't covered, and when you have men on the guards, the center isn't covered. Those uncovered blockers are the ones who can pull on sweeps. But if you bring both men in on the center, they can also go against the guard on their side and so you have two guys taking care of three. In a pass situation, that means your ends always have a one-on-one situation. On wide runs, most teams like to pull their weak-side guard, but they can't against this defense.

"That means there are certain plays you can't run against this defense. You take away their guard-pulling plays, their delay plays, a lot of their traps and their play-action passes,

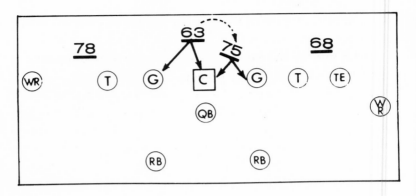

Pittsburgh's Odd 4–3

because you get such good penetration. There are some plays you are vulnerable to, but if you eliminate part of a team's offense you find you only have to concentrate on working against two or three plays a week, and anything you emphasize you're bound to do better."

According to Perles, the Odd 4–3 is most vulnerable to quick-hitting plays up the middle. "But with our people, Fats and Joe at two hundred and seventy-five pounds apiece, you won't kill us with that kind of stuff. If we can make you eliminate all that finesse stuff and run right at us, we should win the game."

The new defense helped eliminate Joe Greene's biggest weakness. Because of his quickness and speed, he had always been vulnerable to traps and sucker and misdirection plays. Because of the quick penetration from both men charging up the middle—especially with Holmes usually a step or two behind to cover up—Greene no longer had to worry about this. These plays would no longer work.

"It made every down for Joe like third-and-fifteen," Perles chortles.

Perles said he started tinkering with the new alignment at midseason merely as a diversion to keep his players from getting bored. "When you've got players as good as they are, things are bound to get boring through a fourteen-game schedule, plus six preseason games," Perles explains. Since defensive line play is so basic, "the first place you notice it is generally in the front four."

So he came up with the basic idea and then asked his players to devise variations and adjustments to make it more effective as an all-around defense. It was first unveiled in full-scale practice as a pass-rush defense to give the offense a "look" when preparing for opponents who used an odd front or did a lot of stunting. (Stunting means that the two tackles or a tackle and an end on the same side loop around each other and exchange pass rush routes to confuse blocking assignments.)

Once the new defense showed it was effective in passing situations, Perles began to think of it in terms of game use, and so he had to see how it would work against the run. He asked backfield coach Dick Hoak to try some running plays against the alignment. It worked. Certain types of plays just would not work against this defense, and Perles and the other defense coaches then made adjustments to compensate in other areas against those that remained effective.

It was a stimulating time for Perles and his front four, all of whom got totally involved in the experiment. There were no complaints about extra time for practice or meetings. "Week after week we spent time searching for weaknesses," Perles says. "In practice, we'd tell Dick Hoak we were going to be in that defense and for him to try to beat it. Sometimes he did hurt us, but it would usually be with plays that were far out, plays that it would be tough for a team to put in just for us.

"We searched and we searched because there was no history, no films for us to study. We worked to try to beat ourselves, and when we did, we would go right back to try to iron things out. It was a real good atmosphere as far as stimulating each other's mind.

"Joe and Fats had a great deal to say about this alignment. They were very proud of it and they guarded it like it was part of them. I'm sure that because of this they all played it better than they probably would have played a conventional defense."

Greene admits he was skeptical at first about the new alignment, but he soon realized he would become its biggest beneficiary. "Because of the way I play, it gives me a chance to cheat a little bit, especially with Ernie there to cover up— and he did a fantastic job of it in the Super Bowl," Joe says.

The key, of course, is really Joe Greene, because of his combination of speed and strength. As Perles pointed out, Greene and Holmes could go all out and yet they were strong enough to compensate and overpower blockers on those quick-hitters.

After the Super Bowl, Noll was asked if he thought other teams might copy the Steelers' Odd 4–3. "I doubt it," he said with a smile. "To do it, they would have to have someone like Joe Greene."

Perles says the new defense was used a couple of times midway in the season when games already were safely won. It was tried for a half against Kansas City, then discarded until the New England game, a most important contest since it came after the Houston loss. It was used virtually all the way in that game as the Steelers won to clinch their division title and a spot in the playoffs for the third straight year.

The Odd 4–3 was polished in a closing victory over Cincinnati, and then, says Perles, "We sold out to it for the playoffs."

The result would be one of the most awesome defensive displays over a three-game series in playoff history.

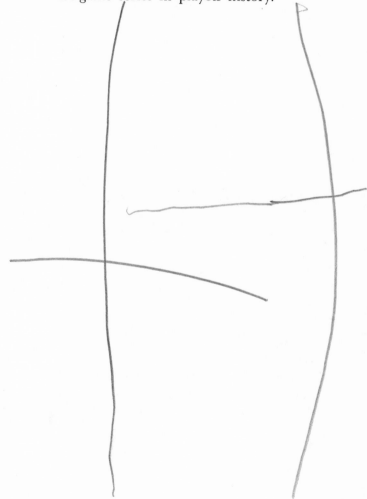

11

One for the Chief

The Pittsburgh Steelers were scheduled to open the 1974 playoffs on Sunday, December 22, in Three Rivers Stadium against Buffalo, the wild card contestant. Their psychological road to the Super Bowl would start a day earlier. On Saturday, in the other half of the American Conference draw, the defending champion Miami Dolphins met the Raiders in Oakland. These two teams generally were rated the strongest in football. Many called this game "the real Super Bowl."

The game did turn out to be a classic. Oakland won, 28–26, on Clarence Davis's dramatic diving end-zone catch of an eight-yard pass from Ken Stabler with eight seconds to play. Less than two minutes earlier, the Dolphins had taken a seemingly safe lead on a twenty-three-yard touchdown run by Benny Malone.

Most of the Steelers watched this game. Despite the defeat, Joe Greene remained firm in his admiration for the Dolphins, a team that had won two straight Super Bowls and had reached a contending position in the playoffs twice more in the last four seasons. He noted how the Dolphins' famous

"53" defense had done them in at the end. The "53" is not noted for its strong pass rush and, given that time, Oakland quarterback Ken Stabler was able to maneuver his team in range for the winning touchdown. Ironically, he threw that pass while being dragged down by a Miami pass rusher. There was no such "53" subtlety in Pittsburgh's pass rush. It was tee off and *pow!* by Pittsburgh.

The course of the game, however, was not what most impressed the Steelers. All through the telecast, Oakland coach John Madden was quoted to the affect that "anything can happen when the two best teams in football meet." The Steelers bristled at this suggestion that they were no better than number three. None bristled more than Chuck Noll. He would remember that quote—and use it.

Buffalo, once an American Football League power, was getting back into the playoffs for the first time in eight years, and the Bills had achieved this revival on the winged heels of O. J. Simpson, pro football's most dangerous running back.

Despite their awesome defensive reputation, the Steelers knew stopping Simpson would not be easy. In fact, their defensive philosophy was made to order for the Juice. Pittsburgh's defense was a come-at-you, hell-for-leather sort of thing. O. J. loved defenders who came at him full blast. It was an easy matter for him to change direction, pick up the pace, and dart into the distance, leaving would-be tacklers sprawling and clutching air. He had his biggest problems with containment teams like Miami, disciplined groups that stood their ground and made him come to them. He openly looked forward to playing against the Steelers front four.

As the Steelers prepared their defensive strategy, they

knew they had to control some of their aggressive instincts.

Some Steelers worried about this game simply because they were heavily favored. They had expected to be tested the week before in the season's windup against Cincinnati, a bitter division rival. However, that game had proved meaningless when Pittsburgh clinched its division championship the week before. The Bengals, decimated by injury, put up little fight.

O. J. Simpson frightened Dwight White and many of the other Steelers. "We can beat them," White though that week, "but if we go out there messing around, we can lose." He was worried because "Cincinnati had come in and died on us and now we have to stay pumped up ourselves and mentally on track for another week."

The Steelers had led the NFL with fifty-two quarterback sacks, and this forced the Bills to make a major change in their strategy. Joe Ferguson, their young quarterback, had been a straight drop-back passer all season. Against the Steelers, coach Lou Saban thought the kid from Terry Bradshaw's home town (and high school) would have to roll out so as not to present a stationary target. The Steelers smiled when they saw this. It's more difficult to pass accurately on the run, and of course any time you make a team depart from its usual approach, it's a plus.

The Bills actually led, 7–3, after the first period, but Pittsburgh exploded for twenty-six points in the second quarter and that was it. "They blew us out of the tub and forced us to abandon our game plan," Saban complained after the 32–14 rout was completed.

Once Pittsburgh got its big lead, the Bills no longer could content themselves with their usual offense of O. J. left, O. J.

right, and O. J. up the middle. They had to throw the ball. Although Ferguson was not sacked once, the threat of that Pittsburgh pass rush made him ineffective.

There were two significant developments in this game worth noting by future Steeler opponents. For one thing, Pittsburgh, for the first time all year, showed a devastating offense. The Bills later said this was the difference, the dimension they had not expected from a team that previously had been carried by its defensive platoon. Franco Harris scored a playoff record three touchdowns; Lynn Swann, an engaging rookie from Southern Cal who had once baby-sat for O. J. Simpson's kids in Los Angeles, caught important passes and gained big yardage on two end-around runs; and Terry Bradshaw played perhaps his best game at quarterback since coming out of Louisiana Tech five years earlier.

He was sharp, he was accurate, he was in complete command of the game plan. He completed twelve of nineteen passes for 203 yards and one touchdown. He was not intercepted. He did not panic. And he ran five times for forty-eight yards, a talent that Noll now said was one reason he had eventually decided to settle on Bradshaw as his quarterback late in the season. Maybe, just maybe, what Joe Greene had hoped was coming true. Terry Bradshaw was growing up with the team.

The second factor was the way the Bills kept Simpson under control. The previous season he had gained an all-time pro record 2,003 yards. This year, despite ankle and knee problems, he ran for over a thousand. On this afternoon he gained only forty-nine yards on fifteen carries. His longest run was eleven yards. The front four had sacrificed some of its pass rush to play containment against Simpson, and it worked. They knew they would have completely stifled an ordinary back. That Simpson had gained as many as forty-nine yards was a complete demonstration of his ability. Even his small gainers left them gasping because they should have been losses. The Bills as a team managed only one hundred yards rushing.

As they left Three Rivers Stadium, Joe Greene told his wife that O. J. Simpson had gained only forty-nine yards that afternoon.

"If you can hold O. J. Simpson under fifty yards," said Agnes Greene, "nothing can stop you now."

O. J. Simpson, who also had seen the previous day's Oakland-Miami game on television, picked the Steelers to beat Oakland the following week.

Playing the Raiders is never merely a game for Pittsburgh, it is a crusade. Chuck Noll stepped out of character when he greeted his players the Tuesday after they defeated Buffalo.

For the first time most of his players could remember, he was emotional in discussing an upcoming opponent.

"I watched that game on TV, too," he reminded them. "I heard that stuff about what Madden said about 'when the two best teams in football get together.' Well, I thought that's what the playoffs were for. I thought the Super Bowl was to decide who the best team in football was.

"Well, the two best teams in football didn't play that game," Noll continued, his voice getting harsher. "When we played them last time, we weren't playing our game. But we got something for them this week. The best team is going to the Super Bowl and it's going to be us. Neither one of them is going to be going!"

Hey, that ain't Chuck, Joe Greene thought as his coach presented this emotional appeal, which naturally was all the more effective because it was so unusual. If the Steelers had played Oakland five minutes after Chuck's speech, they would have won, 100–0.

Later Joe Greene would look back and say, "The Oakland game was won by Chuck Noll that Tuesday."

In Dwight White's words, the remaining days before the Steelers met Oakland added up to "a real sticky week, I mean the air was really thick everywhere we went."

He added, "You know, we had already suffered that humiliation in the early part of the season. We knew we'd beaten these people before with the same personnel, the same offensive plays, the same people running the ball. We'd beaten them twice, we'd lost to them twice, and now what were we going to do?

"Well, this time we were not going to be blocked, this time we were determined to beat them. We would make up for all the others. We were playing them on their home field, where they had all the advantages, but we were going to beat them for all the cookies."

As they prepared for this game, George Perles kept reminding his players how an Oakland cornerback had scornfully pointed to the scoreboard as the clock ticked down for the final seconds of that 17–0 humiliation in Pittsburgh.

The Steelers thought about their rivalry with Oakland and why it had become such a bitter thing.

"Oakland's the type of team that likes to beat the hell out of you if you just go out there messing around, and nobody likes to be embarrassed," Joe Greene explained. "Then there are all those sly things they like to do. In '73, that guy did have grease on him. We know we've got to play a good game, because Oakland at Oakland is always tough. Watching Oakland-Miami I was scared to death."

"There's no bad feeling," Dwight White insisted, "just vicious competitiveness. I really respect the hell out of them. Pittsburgh and Oakland are the two best teams in football and I think they respect us, too. The competition is so keen that you have to assume there is some kind of bad feeling, but Art Shell and I spend time together in the off-season, and Gene Upshaw, too.

"But on the football field, they like to play us and we like to play them and we end up destroying each other. It's the complete annihilation of both teams. You know, if I don't protect myself, you'll kick me until I say stop or until I make you say stop. One of my college coaches used to say when we played Texas A. & I., 'Now dammit, men, they'll run it up to a hundred if you let 'em. They won't try to keep from embarrassing you.' That's the way it is with Oakland.

"If you beat me, so what, it's just a game," White concluded. "But don't humiliate me. It's like when a guy beats you for a touchdown and then bangs the ball down in front of you. You feel like choking him to death."

Ernie Holmes's approach to the game was simplistic. "I've got revenge in my mind. They came in and whupped us on our home court and we lost to them the last time [in the playoffs]. Gene Upshaw is my very good friend, but all I can see is knocking him out."

L. C. Greenwood had watched Oakland-Miami with mixed feelings. "I really wanted to play against Oakland, although for the team it would have been best if we played Miami because we'd have gotten them at home," L. C. explained. "See, I've got a personal thing with Oakland. We've been getting a lot of raw deals from them the last two-three years, plus I've had a few run-ins with their offensive tackle. I like to play against people who don't try to take advantage of you in a foul way. I don't like dirty play and I think I play a pretty decent game myself. But I'd played against John Vella a couple of times and it seemed each time he'd do something he didn't have to do, like clip me or go at me from behind or grab me when I was rushing the passer."

A game with Oakland wouldn't be complete without some kind of incident. The night before, several Steelers were robbed as they slept in their hotel rooms. Terry Bradshaw, who half awakened during the robbery, lost $60 and some credit cards. Ron Shanklin was taken for $100. Lynn Swann awoke during the theft and chased the robbers, two girls, out of his room. He didn't pursue them. "Any lady bold enough to walk into a hotel room where Joe Greene is liable to be sleeping is bold enough to be carrying a gun or a knife," Swann said wisely.

He called the front desk and one of the robbers' apparent accomplices was apprehended. She was carrying 133 room keys for the hotel. None of the loot was recovered, but, as Bradshaw said, "Thank God nobody got hurt."

This was one incident the Steelers didn't blame on Al Davis and the Raiders.

Once before Pittsburgh had come this close to the Super Bowl. Two years earlier the Steelers had lost to Miami for the conference championship. Were they in danger of developing an Oakland reputation for losing the big ones?

As the team was leaving its hotel to head for the stadium,

Joe Green ran into Art Rooney in the hall. "We're gonna get them," Greene reassured his white-haired employer who had known so many disappointments over the year. Rooney was convinced.

"Joe had been giving me confidence all through the year," Rooney said. "In fact, way back when he was a rookie, he kept telling me we were going to have a good team someday."

Oakland's victory over Miami was still strong in Rooney's mind, however. He had only one worry as he headed for the stadium, that Oakland might be able to go ahead in the final minutes of the game and the Steelers would not have time to retaliate.

It was a heavy scene from the moment the Steelers walked out on the field to be greeted by the jeers of thousands of Oakland fans. The defensive linemen took their warmups in the end zone and Raider partisans taunted them from close range. "L. C. is a cow" was one of the printable epithets. They waved their black handkerchiefs and George Perles could see anger coming to a boil in his players. When angry, his front four were unstoppable. "Keep it up, keep it up," he challenged the fans, egging them on. They were doing his job for him.

Despite their confidence, the Steelers started slowly. They gave Oakland a field goal on Lynn Swann's fumble, Roy Gerela missed a twenty-yard field-goal attempt, one of the officials blew the call and disallowed what should have been a Pittsburgh touchdown pass, and another Steeler pass was intercepted near the goal line.

Early in the game, the Steelers' defensive coaches got another scare. Woody Widenhofer, one of the assistants, was up in the press box, and as he looked down at the Raider bench he spotted coaches with a blackboard and the offensive unit huddled around them. A coach obviously was diagramming plays. Widenhofer was dismayed. He screamed into the telephone set clamped to his head, "They've got a chalkboard, they're getting plays together!"

The Steelers were afraid that the Raiders had come up with a reading on their Odd 4–3 defense and were plotting strategy to destroy it. Should the Steelers get out of it and return to a more conventional defense? They seriously considered such a move because they still were apprehensive about the new alignment. "We had no experience with it, we were afraid they'd hurt us," Perles recalls. But then the decision was made: Let 'em hurt us first, then we can change. "Sometimes," Perles confesses, "you tend to give the other team too much credit."

Oakland led after the first quarter, 3–0. It was 3–3 at the half and 10–3, Oakland, after three quarters.

By the final period, however, the Steeler defense finally was beginning to get to Oakland quarterback Ken Stabler. He was throwing on the run under severe pressure. And the relentless Steeler ground game was beating Oakland's front four into submission. In that final quarter Franco Harris scored two touchdowns and Lynn Swann caught a Bradshaw pass for a third as Pittsburgh added twenty-one points for a 24–13 victory.

When it was over, Harris showed 111 yards rushing. Rocky Bleier, the Viet Nam war hero who played because of his blocking, sometimes was known as a third guard in the Pittsburgh offense. On this day he was a runner with ninety-eight yards rushing. And Bradshaw had another superb game. He had stuck with Noll's game plan for basic football, throwing only 17 times for eight completions. He had called plays perfectly. As the Steelers headed for the Super Bowl, Noll praised Bradshaw as being "at the peak of his game."

Meanwhile, on the other side of the stat sheet, Stabler was flinging the ball thirty-six times for nineteen completions. He was intercepted three times and sacked twice.

The Raiders, with Stabler at quarterback, a huge offensive line, and a fine stable of running backs, have developed into a ball control team. They like to ram it down your throat, use up the clock, beat up on you physically.

But on this afternoon they could muster only twenty-nine yards rushing. It was an incredible defensive performance. Clarence Davis, perhaps Oakland's most dangerous breakaway threat, carried ten times and had only sixteen yards to show for it. Marv Hubbard, an all-star fullback, averaged less than a yard per carry. The Raiders' longest run from scrimmage was four yards.

"We've been striving to find out who we were all season long and now we know," Joe Greene said solemnly in the dressing room. "We are a damn good football team because we beat a damn good football team."

Given the emotional climate of this game, the Oakland victory ranks virtually on a par with their subsequent Super Bowl triumph. "The Super Bowl doesn't take a back seat to any game, but only because it's the Super Bowl," Joe Greene said weeks after the season. "I'll never forget the playoff game with Oakland. It accounted for a lot of things and it was played with such intensity, such feeling. Everybody was hooked up on the same wavelength, the whole squad. There was no way we were going to lose that game.

When the Steelers subsequently ordered their Super Bowl victory rings, they made sure the design included all three playoff scores. That was one way they could be sure the satisfying victory over Oakland was commemorated.

Now it was on to the Super Bowl. Earlier in the afternoon, the Minnesota Vikings had beaten Los Angeles 14–10 for the National Conference championship. The Vikings had played and lost in the Super Bowl twice before, including the previous January to Miami.

They would have two weeks to prepare for this game. Surely, Pittsburgh coaches felt, the Vikings would be able to devise tactics to take advantage of the Odd 4–3 defense. Again they considered abandoning the new alignment. Again they decided, "Let 'em hurt us first." However, just in case, they worked on two defensive strategies. They would go into the Super Bowl with Plan A and Plan B.

Except for the disquieting developments concerning Dwight White's illness, the Steelers enjoyed most of their week in New Orleans before the Super Bowl. But as they came off the field for those final moments in the dressing room before the kickoff, they suddenly seemed struck by the awesomeness of the occasion.

They fell silent. Tension began to fill the cramped room. Suddenly Glen (Pine) Edwards jumped to his feet. "Hey, what are we sitting around for like this?" he demanded.

The tension evaporated in yells and laughter. The Steelers were themselves again. Chuck Noll began to speak.

"This is the big one," he said simply. "This is the game we've been pointing to since August when camp opened. I've got the utmost confidence in you and I feel you're ready to play. It's up to you now to go out and do the job. The team that wants it most today is going to win."

Then he added, "It would be a lot of fun to win this game, so let's go out and have some fun."

It was pure, vintage Noll. He had made his emotional pitch two and a half weeks earlier.

It had been raining most of the morning in New Orleans, but it stopped just before the kickoff and a stiff north wind was whipping the length of the field. Flags atop the stadium fluttered away from their poles. Pittsburgh won the coin toss, which actually is held half an hour before the game, and elected to receive. Minnesota, with its choice of goals, opted to defend the south end of the stadium with the wind in its face.

Fran Tarkenton, the Viking quarterback, was dumfounded. He had been playing most of the season with a sore arm. He didn't have the most powerful arm in the world anyway, and later he would say the injury had left him 60 percent effective. He needed all the help he could get, and he had to open the game by throwing into the wind. Noll also couldn't believe the Steelers' good fortune, but he accepted it graciously. In the press box, at least one newsman recalled Abner Haynes's celebrated gaffe in an overtime playoff for the American Football League championship in 1962. After that coin toss to start the extra period, Haynes, captain of the old Dallas Texans, had said, "We'll kick to the wind." His team ended up with neither ball nor the wind, a critical factor in a sudden-death situation. That error had been made under extreme pressure by a flustered player. What was Bud Grant's excuse? "I didn't think the wind was a factor," he deadpanned after the game.

The course of the game, however, may very well have been decided by that blunder. The Steelers received the kickoff, but were unable to move on their first series of downs as first Franco Harris and then Bradshaw slipped on the wet Poly-Turf. While Bradshaw was changing his shoes for better traction, Bobby Walden came off the bench for his first punt. He got off a boomer that caught the wind and soared fifty-two yards deep into Viking territory.

Minnesota was forced to set up on offense inside its own twenty-yard line. The Vikings would spend the rest of the quarter with their backs to the wall. Their offense would be limited. The Pittsburgh front four would be free to tee off with abandon and thus establish critical individual domi-nance in the trenches. Minnesota probably wouldn't have won the game anyway, but the Vikings may have been doomed to defeat thirty minutes before the kickoff with that stupid choice of goals.

On first down, as if to establish that his arm wasn't that sore, Fran Tarkenton passed sixteen yards to John Gilliam. He passed incomplete to Stu Voight and then sent Dave Os-born cracking over left guard into Dwight White's territory. White stopped him for a yard gain. For the rest of the first quarter, the ailing defensive end, just out of a hospital bed, would be tested only twice more. Again the Steelers were dumfounded.

The Vikings had known all week that Pittsburgh would have either a sick man or a slow substitute at right end. They had time to work on a whole series of plays designed either to wear White down or to take advantage of Steve Furness's inexperience.

Instead, the Vikings stuck with the basic right-handed offense that had carried them this far. The year before, Miami fullback Larry Csonka had been named the Super Bowl's most valuable player for his performance against Minnesota. In accepting his award, he said, ". . . and I want to thank Minnesota and Bud Grant for staying in the same four–three [defense] all game."

As Super Bowl IX progressed through the first period, the Steelers were struck by the predictability of Minnesota's offense. The Odd 4–3 as planned had taken away many of the Vikings' plays, especially the sweeps by dangerous Chuck Foreman. Briefed well by Perles and defensive coordinator Bud Carson, the Steelers knew in given situations virtually every play the Vikings would run. The tip-off was the formation. Osborn, for instance, they recalled later, carried the ball himself only when the backs were split. As Tarkenton called signals and the plays developed, the front four could see George Perles's blackboard X's come to life.

Dwight White was especially surprised by the way the first period developed. Each time he came off the field, he was surrounded by teammates, coaches, and the medical staff, all inquiring as to his health. Yet when he went back out on the field, the Vikings virtually ignored him. "I thought they'd open the gates on me," he said afterward. "I thought they'd come at me until they had to stretcher me off the field." Instead, the Vikes ran only three plays to the left side of the line in the whole first period. They gained two yards. On the last play of the first quarter, White stopped Osborn for no gain. As the game progressed, White stopped everything in his direction. He played well even for a man who was not ill and he missed only one series in the fourth quarter with a pinched nerve that had nothing to do with his pneumonia. Afterward, a TV interviewer gushed, "You sure don't look sick." "Well, I feel sick," White replied.

The first period was scoreless but Pittsburgh dominance already was established. The Vikings were held to zero yards rushing. Their only first down had come on Tarkenton's first play. They hadn't even reached midfield. The Steelers, meanwhile, had totaled seventy-nine yards in total offense and had gotten close enough for Roy Gerela to attempt two field goals from reasonably close range. One he missed, the other was aborted by a bad snap.

The second quarter started out as a replay of the first, although Minnesota did get a scoring shot, thanks to Rocky Bleier's fumble. However, Fred Cox missed a thirty-nine-yard field-goal attempt.

The Steelers now were able to drive back across midfield before they punted, and Walden boomed another that Minnesota fielded at its seven for no return.

As he trotted out on the field with the rest of the defense, L. C. Greenwood was thinking what a lovely spot for a safety. The Vikings would try to punch it out on the first two downs. If the Steelers held, they might be able to nail Tarkenton on third down when he tried to pass out of his end zone.

On first down, Chuck Foreman hit left tackle and gained three yards to the ten. Greenwood's dreams of a safety began to fade. But on the next play he saw the play developing in his direction. Tarkenton spun to hand off to Osborn running right. Osborn never got the ball. Perhaps Tarkenton hit himself in the leg with the ball, perhaps he saw Greenwood's quick penetration and tried to pull the ball back. In any case, the handoff was botched and L. C. saw it all in front of him like a slow-motion movie. He crashed into the empty-handed Osborn and also smacked the loose ball with his shoulder, sending it bouncing swiftly back toward the end zone. If a Steeler fell on the ball, it would be a Pittsburgh touchdown; if it was covered by a Viking over the goal line, it would be a two-point safety. Tarkenton, Greenwood, Dwight White, and rookie linebacker Jack Lambert led the mad race for the football and Fran got there first. He had hoped to down the ball before it crossed the line so Minnesota would have a chance to punt out of danger, but it slid into the end zone just as he fell on it. White, who later said, "I've been around long enough to know not to go ape in a situation like that," reached over and touched Tarkenton, which was sufficient to kill the play. Then the rookie, Lambert, fell on him to make sure as Mike Wagner triumphantly signaled safety.

Not quite as planned, L. C. Greenwood had gotten his safety. With just under seven and a half minutes left in the second quarter, the Steelers led, 2–0. L. C. began to think what a tribute it would be to the defense if that turned out to be the final score.

The Vikings didn't get to the Super Bowl by being push-overs, however. They got their free kick after the safety, forced a Pittsburgh punt, and then, as the half drew to a close, drove for the first time under their own power into Steeler territory. On first down from Pittsburgh's twenty-five, Tarkenton spotted John Gilliam, like L. C. Greenwood a WFL lame duck who was determined to go out in style, at the five. The pass was a little high, but in reach of the leaping Gilliam. However, as Gilliam started to pull the ball down, Glen Edwards came charging up and punched it out of his hands with both fists. The ball flew back up in the air and Mel Blount intercepted at the goal line.

Art Rooney watched impassively from his box on the fifty-yard line as the Steelers ran out the clock on one of the most one-sided 2–0 halves most of the witnesses had ever seen. Rooney never cheers during a ball game and can't abide sitting with people who do. That's one reason he prefers to watch most games from the working press area with his friends the sports writers.

Before the game, Rooney had been holding court in the press box when Max Winter, dapper but shy president of the Vikings, passed by. Rooney and Winter were old friends, from the years when both promoted prizefights. But Winter was a comparative newcomer to pro football, and ever since they both had arrived in New Orleans late in the week, Rooney had been unintentionally upstaging him. Rooney was even more embarrassed by this than Winter.

As Max spotted his old friend holding an informal press conference, he called out in a joshing tone, "Not yet, not yet."

Rooney, however, for perhaps the first time in his sporting life, was supremely confident about this game. In past years, whenever anyone asked him how his team or one of his horses was going to fare, he'd answer cautiously, "I hope we win." This week, when asked the same question before a mob of reporters at press headquarters, he replied, "We're going to win." Waiting for lightning to strike him dead for this presumption, Art wondered if newsmen who had known him intimately over the years had noticed the subtle difference in his reply. He knew he'd never have said anything like that about one of his horses.

At half time, as statistics were being passed out to show

the Vikings had managed to gain only eleven yards rushing, television people spotted Rooney and asked him to drop down to the area where they planned to do the postgame show. They wanted to check camera angles or something. At the same time, a stripper from the French Quarter, scantily clad despite the chill weather, had raced out on the field to join the half-time show. On their way to the creaking press-box elevator, Rooney spotted Winter and asked him to join the group. Max, fearful of hexing his team, declined. Rooney twitted him about preferring to watch the strip-teaser. "What are you looking at, you've seen that for fifty years," Rooney teased his white-haired friend.

"No, I'm not going down. Go down yourself," Winter insisted.

Rooney wasn't worried about jinxing his team. He knew luck is on the side of the toughest tackles.

Even though the score was only 2–0, most of the Steelers were supremely confident, although few would admit it, even now. The scenario reminded some of the Oakland game where they dominated a first half that had been close only on the scoreboard. In both games, Joe Greene spent the first half roaming the sidelines, mostly when the special teams were on the field. He spent his time encouraging the offense. "Come on, you guys, keep plugging," he cheered them. "Don't worry about a thing. You're gonna score, and we're gonna hold them."

Six years after Dan Rooney had encouraged him to take over that role, Joe Greene was acting as a team leader by word as well as example. Even in the heat of battle, Ralph Berlin, the trainer who had known him from the beginning, was struck by the change.

The second-half kickoff seemed to decree that this would be Pittsburgh's day. Minnesota would have the ball and the wind, and good field position, too, because Roy Gerela stubbed his toe and squibbed the kick. So what happened? Bill Brown had trouble handling the ball, he fumbled, and Pittsburgh recovered at Minnesota's thirty.

Four plays later, the Steelers scored on a nine-yard run by Franco Harris. Gerela converted for a 9–0 lead.

The Steelers could see Minnesota bending in the third quarter, like an arm wrestler whose wrist is gradually being forced to the table. Joe Greene was smashing into the backfield and intercepted a pass. L. C. Greenwood was looming up in front of Tarkenton like the Tower of Pisa every time Francis tried to roll out in his direction. Like an imperious traffic cop stopping traffic, he batted down three Tarkenton passes all by himself. Dwight White, defying medical science, was playing so well that the Vikes abandoned whatever plans they may have considered for attacking his area. Ernie Holmes was a rock in the middle. Tarkenton never was thrown for a loss while passing, but the Steelers were punishing him. They took away his basic plays. He started throwing what White called "that short dinky stuff."

He's tired of getting hit, White thought to himself.

Tarkenton's frustration became apparent. He's a talker on the field, and for a minister's son playing the noncombat role of quarterback, he gets into more than his share of altercations. His mouth must be the reason. As he walked off the field when the punting team came on, he was cursing his teammates and goading them in his high-pitched Georgia drawl. We got him, White thought as he noted Tarkenton's cursin' and fussin'.

Tarkenton wasn't the only frustrated Viking. Up and down the line, the Vikes were jabbering at the Steelers. No outright insults, just conversation calculated to get them upset, get them off their game. John Gilliam was jawing at Glen Edwards, but mostly the Steelers worried about Joe Greene. They always watched Joe Greene in a game. He has that explosive temper. They didn't want him beheading anybody. They couldn't afford the fifteen-yard penalty and they certainly never wanted him thrown out of a game. In this situation, the tables are turned in the front four. The other three become protective of Joe Greene.

As the yapping continued, the Steelers tried to compose themselves. The more they tried to cool it, though, the more excited they got. Joe Greene tried to close it down. They told him to shut up, too.

Finally, the Steelers heard a strange voice. L. C. Greenwood had been getting angry at all the conversation. The Vikings weren't even on the scoreboard and here they were succeeding in agitating the team that was winning. "All right, let's cut it out. Let's be cool," he suggested. The Steelers were dumfounded. L. C. Greenwood never opened his mouth on the field, or, generally, in any kind of open forum. But this unexpected reprimand proved just as effective as Noll's uncharacteristic pep talk before the Oakland game. As the Steelers settled down to play ball again, Greenwood confidently thought to himself. The case is closed.

At least one Viking had not been trying to stir things up. Mick Tinglehoff, the Minnesota center, didn't want to make anybody mad. Ernie Holmes and Joe Greene had been pounding on him all day. "Man, what's got into you guys?" the old pro asked admiringly. "You guys really came to play today." Ernie Holmes's gold-capped tooth flashed a wicked grin in reply. He was really enjoying this day. He would be sorry when it had to end.

Fate continued to frown on the Vikings. As the fourth quarter began, Mike Wagner was called for pass interference against Gilliam and Minnesota was given a first down on the Steeler five. But on the very next play, Chuck Foreman fumbled when he was speared by Holmes, and Joe Greene recovered at the seven. It was Joe's second big play, and later Chuck Noll would call it the most important defensive play of the game.

The Minnesota threat was only temporarily blunted, however, and at last the Vikings reaped a benefit from Dwight White's illness. When it looked as if Steve Furness would have to play most of the game at defensive end, Chuck Noll relieved him from most of the specialty teams. A veteran who had seen duty there some years before took his place as a blocker when Walden went in to punt. The assignments by now were unfamiliar, however. He took the wrong man and Matt Blair blew in to block Walden's punt from the Steeler fifteen. Terry Brown recovered in the end zone and the Vikings at last were on the board. Fred Cox blew the extra point when his kick bounced off the left upright, but the Vikings were back in the ball game. They trailed by only 9–6 with ten and a half minutes left to play. They could win with a touchdown, tie and force an overtime with a field goal.

Ironically, while the blocked punt marked Minnesota's high-water mark on the scoreboard, the Steelers felt a strange serenity after that score.

"We've got the kind of team that responds to pressure.

We were hungry and desperate to win. I knew Minnesota was in for a heckuvan afternoon after they blocked that punt," said L. C. Greenwood.

On the sidelines, Joe Greene experienced the same eerie feeling. Now that the game was close again, the Steelers were fated to win.

"It was odd, odd, odd," he related afterward. "But I felt the strongest about winning the game when they blocked that punt."

Greene and Greenwood knew their teammates. Minnesota kicked off and the Steeler offense moved to the attack to protect their lead. Bradshaw, who was brilliant for the third playoff game in a row, slowly worked his team downfield. One run after another was called to use up the clock. Twice on third down he had to pass to keep the drive alive. Twice he was successful.

As the clock ticked away, league functionaries collected Art Rooney and escorted him to the dressing room. The best way to get there was to go outside the stadium, around, and back in. As the party ducked back under the stands, they heard a tremendous roar. Maybe it was wishful thinking, but Rooney figured it had the ring of a Pittsburgh cheer. Then a fan wearing a wool hat in Pittsburgh's gold and black came dashing out. "What happened?" Rooney demanded. "We scored! It's all over!" the happy fan screamed.

Rooney remembered another Pittsburgh victory when he had failed to see the final touchdown, but this time there was no agonizing wait to learn if the score would count. On his third third-down situation of the drive, using a play that had been suggested on the sidelines by Joe Gilliam, Bradshaw rolled out and completed a four-yard scoring pass to tight end Larry Brown in the end zone. The score was now 16–6 with barely three and a half minutes left to play. Bradshaw had used up seven full minutes on the clock for this clinching touchdown. At this point even the disciplined Chuck Noll allowed himself to relax and think that perhaps the victory was in hand. Art Rooney, after all those years of waiting, relaxed, too. "We were home."

He stood in the dressing room, still bundled untidily against the cold, a happy old man with a big cigar. As he waited for his boys to come trooping in, he disappeared for a moment into the washroom. He reappeared without his checked cap and explained, "I wanted to make sure my hair was combed."

Once again, as in the Immaculate Reception game, the first player in was punter Bobby Walden. Once again Walden grabbed the Chief in a bear hug and whirled him around. "Well, we did it," Walden said with emotion if not much poetry.

The Steelers knelt for a prayer of thanksgiving, and Chuck Noll said, "I can't think of anything more appropriate than our defensive team shutting them out in a championship game."

Andy Russell, the defensive captain, leaped forward to present the game ball. "This one's for the Chief," he shouted. "It's been a long time coming."

"Thank you," Rooney replied. "I'm proud of you and grateful to you."

Sam Davis, the offensive captain, then stepped up. He brandished another football. "And this one is for Coach Noll," he said.

There were no ice cubes in these Steelers' veins at this

moment. "Hip-hip hooray, hip-hip hooray," they cheered,
corny but appropriate, and one by one they came by to shake
Art Rooney's hand. Privately, Rooney was extraproud of his
boys because of the dignified way they handled the victory.
He hadn't felt it necessary to say anything, but he was glad
there was no wild celebration, no throwing of people into
showers, no dousing with champagne. The Steelers went to
the winner's circle like thoroughbreds.

Embarrassed at all the attention, Art Rooney followed his
league escorts to a special press tent where he joined Noll
and his players for postgame interviews.

"This is the biggest win in my life," he said simply. "The
fans of Pittsburgh thought it would be no contest, but I
know that any time you go out there you are eligible to lose."

Epilogue

The party was over. The lights had been flashed on and off for the last time and the players and the coaches and their wives, the reporters and the hangers-on, the friends-of-friends and the gate crashers had long since gone.

At the Fountainebleu Hotel, whatever glamour had existed the night before was stripped away by the harsh Monday-morning sunlight. The lobby was still gritty underfoot with the debris from a thousand celebrants, one or two of whom still slept awkwardly in armchairs.

The world champion Pittsburgh Steelers were packing to return home from their Super Bowl triumph to what they knew would be a rowdy welcome. Sleepy-eyed, somewhat stiff (the usual gait of most football players after a tough game), two by two they crossed the lobby. They carried suitcases, garment bags, and, awkwardly, paper sacks of souvenirs. A fleet of buses was ready to take them to the airport, where two huge jets waited to take them home. Art Rooney had invited scores of old cronies to share this moment. Now it was time to collect his friends and go home.

Downtown, Chuck Noll was on the dais for his final press conference, the last requirement for the winning coach.

He was asked to comment on the Steelers' success. The story, he said, could be told through one man.

"We played our best football all year in the playoffs and this was epitomized by Joe Greene," Noll said of the man who had been his first draft choice back in the dim, grim days of 1-and-13.

"They all stopped running around blockers, they ran right through people to get to the ball," Noll continued. "I never saw the kind of football they played. It was fantastic. And Joe Greene in the playoffs played better than any defensive tackle I have ever seen; probably better than any defensive lineman I have ever seen."

Back in the press room, statisticians were still sorting out the records. At first it was reported that the Steelers had limited Minnesota to twenty-one yards rushing, quite a respectable defensive effort. However, a recheck inspired by Paul Zimmerman of the *New York Post,* whose personal figures proved more accurate than those compiled by a platoon of league specialists, revised this figure downward to a record seventeen yards. Chuck Foreman had produced eighteen yards on a dozen carries. Dave Osborn ended up minus one for eight tries.

In their last two playoff games, the Steelers had held two of the best teams in football to a total of forty-six yards rushing. It was an incredible performance and a tribute strictly to the impregnable front line. If not for O. J. Simpson's acknowledged personal brilliance, the three-game playoff total would have defied belief.

The Steeler front four, who allowed the Vikings only 119

yards in total offense, another all-time low, was the dominant factor of Super Bowl IX. Lynn Swann also set an average punt return record and Franco Harris established Super Bowl highs with thirty-four rushing attempts for 158 yards. Harris was named the game's most valuable player. There is no question that Harris deserved to be honored, but in all probability ticket-splitting had prevented any member of the front four from being named MVP. Any of the four could have been named without embarrassment.

In the aftermath of the game, George Perles felt strangely remorseful. He confessed the Vikings could have been held to even fewer yards if he hadn't made a coaching blunder. The Steelers had been doing well with one of their stunts in passing situations over the first two quarters. At half time, Perles told his boys that the first time Minnesota was in an obvious passing situation, if they called one of their special line stunts, "I guarantee you'll sack him." Well, it came up halfway through the third quarter, third-and-eleven. The Steelers called their stunt, but Fran Tarkenton called a draw play and he sent Chuck Foreman cracking through the vacated hole for a dozen yards.

"I gave up those twelve yards," Perles said mournfully. "If I'd kept my big mouth shut we'd have held them to five yards rushing."

As he prepared to leave for the airport, Dan Rooney was asked about Noll's contract. Noll has a self-extending agreement with the Steelers. Neither he nor Dan knew offhand how many years remained. Rooney indicated that Noll could expect a solid extension that would assure his coaching future in Pittsburgh for many years. If the Steelers ever lost him, it probably would be to a franchise willing to give him a piece of the action.

There was, of course, the usual talk of dynasties. That goes with a Super Bowl victory. The only Steeler players over thirty years of age were guard Sam Davis, center Ray Mansfield, linebacker Andy Russell, and the punter, Bobby Walden. Walden was senior at thirty-six. The Steelers would probably keep him around forever just to hug Art Rooney after big games. Fourteen rookies had made the squad this season, an inordinately high number, but this was because the long strike had cost many fringe veterans their jobs and the roster limit had been boosted from forty to forty-seven.

Noll pointed out that the Steelers also owned NFL rights to a couple of star players from Canada and the WFL who might be jumping back.

"I think down beneath we now know we can compete with the Oaklands and the Miamis. There's no doubt now," said Joe Greene, who pointed out that the true measure of those teams' success was their presence in the playoffs year after year after year.

"They say that when you're champs everybody will try to beat you. Well, I'm glad we're champs, so bring 'em on, bring 'em all on. If we die, we ain't gonna die running. It's gonna be a fight.

"All people have a tendency to get spaced out, to forget what they came from and what they were and how they got where they are. But Pittsburgh's different," he promised. "We've been trying too long to get here."

"We're going to be very dangerous for a lot of people from here on out," Dwight White warned.

But could this exact moment ever be repeated? The first time is always the best, but in the Steelers' case there was an extra dimension that extended beyond just a world championship. For one football season, four men had come together with a perhaps unprecedented singleness of purpose, uniqueness of talent, and commonality of personality.

To borrow Ernie Holmes's favorite figure of speech, four men had stood together in front of the sun and cast a single huge shadow.

It had taken six years, from the hour the Steelers called out Joe Greene's name in the NFL drafting hall, for this combination to come together in this fashion. Would the magic moment last?

As the season ended with the triumph over Minnesota, L. C. Greenwood was within weeks of becoming a free agent. If he didn't jump to the World Football League, he would be free to sign with another team in the NFL. He talked openly of how some other team might be able to build a defense around his talents the way the Steelers had done with Joe Greene. Eventually, he signed again with the Steelers, but how would he react now that his financial hunger was appeased?

What about Ernie Holmes? Soon after the game, he had to appear in a civil suit growing out of the shooting incident. Would he ever truly be free of that cloud? He had signed up with still another attorney and he talked of playing out his option in the 1975 season. He had crossed a picket line and he had turned down, he says, a lucrative WFL offer out of loyalty to the Rooneys. How long could he resist the siren song of instant riches, fame, and fortune still whispered teasingly in his ear?

Joe Greene soon would be approaching thirty years of age himself.

As Dwight White grew intellectually, how long would

football fill all of his needs? How long would he play like a "mad dog"?

To illustrate the fragile nature of this front four, one has only to search for a formal picture of this group. None exists as such in the files of the Pittsburgh Steelers. On picture day before the 1974 season, the first time this foursome was permanently constituted, most of the veterans were on strike. On picture day before the Super Bowl, Dwight White was in the hospital. On another occasion during the season when a formal portrait was scheduled, L. C. Greenwood failed to show.

Elsewhere in this book, we do have a photograph of the four linemen together in uniform. It is not a formal group portrait, it is a contingency shot, and this is reflected in the awkward stances and expressions of the four players involved. It was dug out of the Steelers' file of negatives and it had been taken before the 1973 season. On that picture day, publicity director Joe Gordon ordered three different shots of the front four, one with Ernie Holmes, another with Steve Furness, a third with Tom Keating as the right tackle. There is no sense of togetherness in this picture.

Chuck Noll likes to point out, "There is no security in pro football." Age and injury wield a wicked scythe. Dynasties crumble and the fall is usually all the more striking when championship rosters are allowed to stagnate. Expansion is ahead, too. Which old Steelers would be sacrificed to the new teams?

The front four knows all this. They treasure their season of victory and togetherness. In closing each of my interviews with the players, I asked them what this experience had meant to them. Here are their answers:

Ernie Holmes: "Football this year, it's been such a fantastic year it leaves me speechless sometimes. When I was a kid in college, I watched the Purple People Eaters of Minnesota and Merlin Olsen's gang in Los Angeles and I never thought I'd be part of it and here I am. Being part of the Steel Curtain is such a glorious feeling. I like that, the Steel Curtain, I really do. It represents our purpose. You can run through glass, you can run through cloth, but steel you cannot. And here I am, one of the main characters to make it work. The whole structure of our team this year has been togetherness and respect for each other, and we played that way the entire season."

L. C. Greenwood: "I'm not the type of person who's normally satisfied with things, but I saw before the season started we would get in there and we could play together because we are together. We are individuals, but we socialize together and we have fun playing ball. When you do a lot of things together, you get a feel for the next guy. When you've got somebody in there that you've been playing with constantly, you know what they are doing and they know what you are doing and you can go out and do a lot of things that you normally wouldn't try. The last two-three playoff games, we played decent ball. The whole front four."

Dwight White: "The coming together of our front four is going to epitomize teamwork and what the joint effort of a group of men can do. It's one man to another man, each man doing the job and all having the same objective in mind and being able to absorb differences in opinions, differences in personality. This is going to constitute all of these things, plus just four good football players who should be recognized not only for their physical skills but as four men who tried to set good examples and who succeeded in spite of past adversity. You know, we used to be a team of young college bucks, everybody running all over town, always into something. But now we're settling down and trying to make something of our opportunities, something constructive out of our lives."

Joe Greene: "We're good friends and we're close, but we also had to clear those cobwebs. We're adults, but it took a guy like George Perles to help us find these things. It's believing in one another and that's why we reached the heights that we reached. This is the first year of that, of really being together, and it's going to be that way next year, or better, because this is just a beginning. We've still got some years left to work on that but we've established the foundation. We had our hard knocks and ups and downs and at times we screamed at each other and yelled and cursed. But it was all part of trying to pull ourselves together. This is what it's all about, togetherness."

As Joe Greene left to catch his plane for home, he turned to offer one parting thought.

"I would hate," he said, "for what we've accomplished to be forgotten and not to become part of history."

Records Section

224

Records Section

PITTSBURGH STEELERS SUPER BOWL ROSTER

No.	Name	Pos.	Ht.	Wt.	Age	Yr.	College
45	Allen, Jim	CB	6-2	194	22	R	UCLA
20	Bleier, Rocky	RB	5-11	210	28	6	Notre Dame
47	Blount, Mel	CB	6-3	205	26	5	Southern
38	Bradley, Ed	LB	6-2	239	24	3	Wake Forest
12	Bradshaw, Terry	QB	6-3	218	26	5	Louisiana Tech
87	Brown, Larry	TE	6-4	229	25	4	Kansas
50	Clack, Jim	G-C	6-3	250	26	4	Wake Forest
22	Conn, Richard	S	6-0	185	23	R	Georgia
77	Davis, Charlie	DT	6-1	265	22	R	Texas Christian
57	Davis, Sam	G	6-1	255	30	8	Allen
35	Davis, Steve	RB	6-1	218	24	3	Delaware State
73	Druschel, Rick	G-T	6-2	248	22	R	North Carolina St.
27	Edwards, Glen	S	6-0	185	27	4	Florida A&M
64	Furness, Steve	DT-DE	6-4	255	23	3	Rhode Island
86	Garrett, Reggie	WR	6-1	172	22	R	Eastern Michigan
10	Gerela, Roy	K	5-10	185	26	6	New Mexico State
17	Gilliam, Joe	QB	6-2	187	23	3	Tennessee State
71	Gravelle, Gordon	T	6-5	250	25	3	Brigham Young
75	Greene, Joe	DT	6-4	275	27	6	North Texas State
68	Greenwood, L.C.	DE	6-6	245	28	6	Arkansas AM&N
84	Grossman, Randy	TE	6-1	215	20	R	Temple
59	Ham, Jack	LB	6-1	225	25	4	Penn State
5	Hanratty, Terry	QB	6-1	210	26	6	Notre Dame
32	Harris, Franco	RB	6-2	230	24	3	Penn State
46	Harrison, Reggie	RB	5-11	215	24	R	Cincinnati
63	Holmes, Ernie	DT	6-3	260	26	3	Texas Southern
54	Kellum, Marv	LB	6-2	225	22	R	Wichita State
55	Kolb, Jon	T	6-3	262	27	6	Oklahoma State
58	Lambert, Jack	LB	6-4	215	22	R	Kent State
43	Lewis, Frank	WR	6-1	196	27	4	Grambling
56	Mansfield, Ray	C	6-3	260	33	12	Washington
89	McMakin, John	TE	6-3	232	23	3	Clemson
72	Mullins, Gerry	G-T	6-3	244	25	4	Southern Calif.
26	Pearson, Preston	RB	6-1	205	29	8	Illinois
74	Reavis, Dave	T	6-5	250	24	1	Arkansas
34	Russell, Andy	LB	6-2	225	32	10	Missouri
25	Shanklin, Ron	WR	6-1	190	26	5	North Texas St.
31	Shell, Donnie	S-CB	5-11	190	22	R	So. Carolina St.
82	Stallworth, John	WR	6-2	183	22	R	Alabama A&M
88	Swann, Lynn	WR	5-10	178	22	R	Southern Calif.
24	Thomas, J.T.	CB	6-2	196	23	2	Florida State
51	Toews, Loren	LB	6-3	212	22	2	California
23	Wagner, Mike	S	6-1	210	25	4	Western Illinois
39	Walden, Bobby	P	6-0	190	36	11	Georgia
52	Webster, Mike	C-G	6-1	232	22	R	Wisconsin
78	White, Dwight	DE	6-4	255	25	4	East Texas State
62	Wolf, Jim	DE	6-2	230	22	R	Prairie View

Head Coach: Chuck Noll. Assistants: Bud Carson, Dick Hoak, George Perles, Dan Radakovich, Lionel Taylor, Woody Widenhofer.

HOW THEY WERE BUILT

Year	Draft (34)	Trades (3)	Free Agents (9)
1963	LB Andy Russell (No. 16)		
1964		C Ray Mansfield (from Philadelphia)	
1965			
1966			
1967			G Sam Davis
1968	RB Rocky Bleier (No. 16)	P Bobby Walden (from Minnesota)	
1969	DT Joe Greene (No. 1) QB Terry Hanratty (No. 2A) T Jon Kolb (No. 4) DE L.C. Greenwood (No. 10)		G-C Jim Clack
1970	QB Terry Bradshaw (No. 1) WR Ron Shanklin (No. 2) CB Mel Blount (No. 3)	RB Preston Pearson (from Baltimore)	
1971	WR Frank Lewis (No. 1) LB Jack Ham (No. 2) RB Steve Davis (No. 3) T-G Gerry Mullins (No. 4A) DE Dwight White (No. 4B) TE Larry Brown (No. 5) DT Ernie Holmes (No. 8) S Mike Wagner (No. 11)		S Glen Edwards
1972	RB Franco Harris (No. 1) T Gordon Gravelle (No. 2) TE John McMakin (No. 3) LB Ed Bradley (No. 4) DT Steve Furness (No. 5) QB Joe Gilliam (No. 11)		
1973	CB J.T. Thomas (No. 1) T Dave Reavis (No. 5) LB Loren Toews (No. 8A)		
1974	WR Lynn Swann (No. 1) LB Jack Lambert (No. 2) WR John Stallworth (No. 4A) CB Jimmy Allen (No. 4B) C-G Mike Webster (No. 5) DE Jim Wolf (No. 6A) G-T Rick Druschel (No. 6B) DT Charlie Davis (No. 9B)		S Richard Conn WR Reggie Garrett TE Randy Grossman RB Reggie Harrison LB Marv Kellum S-CB Donnie Shell

Waivers (1): K Roy Gerela (1971, from Houston)

SUPER BOWL SUMMARY

DATE January 12, 1975　DAY OF WEEK Sunday　STARTING TIME 2:00 P.M. CST

VISITING TEAM Pittsburgh Steelers　VS. HOME Minnesota Vikings　AT New Orleans (Tulane)

WEATHER Cloudy, cold　TEMPERATURE 46°　WIND AND DIRECTION North 17 mph

OFFICIALS

REFEREE Bernie Ulman	UMPIRE Al Conway	LINE JUDGE Bruce Alford
LINESMAN Ed Marion	BACK JUDGE Ray Douglas	FIELD JUDGE Dick Dolack

LINEUPS

VISITORS

	OFFENSE			DEFENSE	
WR	43	Lewis	LE	68	Greenwood
LT	55	Kolb	LT	75	Greene
LG	50	Clack	RT	63	Holmes
C	56	Mansfield	RE	78	White
RG	72	Mullins	LLB	59	Ham
RT	71	Gravelle	MLB	58	Lambert
TE	87	Brown	RLB	34	Russell
WR	25	Shanklin	LCB	24	Thomas
QB	12	Bradshaw	RCB	47	Blount
RB	20	Bleier	LS	23	Wagner
RB	32	Harris	RS	27	Edwards

SUBSTITUTIONS

OFFENSE: Stallworth, Garrett, Swann, Reaves, Sam Davis, Webster, Druschel, Grossman, McMakin, Pearson, Harrison, Steve Davis. DEFENSE: Furness, Toews, C. Davis, Kellum, Bradley, Allen, Conn, Shell. KICKERS: Walden, Gerela

HOME

	OFFENSE			DEFENSE	
WR	82	Lash	LE	81	Eller
LT	68	Goodrum	LT	69	Sutherland
LG	66	Maurer	RT	88	Page
C	53	Tingelhoff	RE	70	Marshall
RG	62	White	LLB	60	Winston
RT	73	Yary	MLB	50	Siemon
TE	83	Voigt	RLB	58	Hilgenberg
WR	42	Gilliam	LCB	43	N. Wright
QB	10	Tarkenton	RCB	25	Wallace
RB	44	Foreman	LS	23	J. Wright
RB	41	Osborn	RS	22	Krause

SUBSTITUTIONS

OFFENSE: McCullum, Alderman, Anderson, Sunde, Lawson, Kingsriter, Craig, Reed, Marinaro, McClanahan, B. Brown. DEFENSE: Larsen, Lurtsema, Blair, Martin, McNeill, T. Brown, Poltl. KICKERS: Eischeid, Cox

SUPER BOWL SUMMARY, continued

Wolf, Gilliam, Hanratty

DID NOT PLAY

INACTIVE

Berry, Boone, Blahak, Riley, Holland

INDIVIDUAL SCORING

	TOUCHDOWNS	T. Brown
Harris, L. Brown		

P.A.T.'S

Gerela (2)

FIELD GOALS

Gerela (1) — FIELD GOALS MISSED — Cox (1)

	1	2	3	4	TOTAL
	(Visitor)				
PITTSBURGH STEELERS	0	2	7	7	16
	(Home)				
MINNESOTA VIKINGS	0	0	0	6	6

TEAM	PERIOD	ELAPSED TIME	SCORING PLAY	SCORE VISITOR	HOME
PITT.	2	7:49	Safety (White downed Tarkenton in end zone)	2	0
PITT.	3	1:35	Harris 12 run (Gerela kick)	9	0
MINN.	4	4:27	T. Brown Recovered blocked punt (kick failed)	9	6
PITT.	4	11:29	L. Brown 4 pass from Bradshaw (Gerela kick)	16	6

ATTENDANCE 80,997 (Paid) 79,065 (Actual)   TIME OF GAME 2:56

FINAL INDIVIDUAL STATISTICS

PITTSBURGH STEELERS

RUSHING	ATT.	NET YDS.	AVG.	LONG GAIN	TD
Bleier	17	65	3.8	18	0
Harris	34	158	4.6	25	1
Bradshaw	5	33	6.6	17	0
Swann	1	−7	−7.0	−7	0
TOTALS	57	249	4.4	25	1

PASSING	ATT.	COMP.	YDS.	TKD	YDS.	TD	LG.	Had Int.
Bradshaw	14	9	96	2	12	1	30	0
TOTALS	14	9	96	2	12	1	30	0

PASS RECEIVING	NO.	YDS.	LG.	TD
Lewis	1	12	12	0
Brown	3	49	30	1
Stallworth	3	24	22	0
Bleier	2	11	6	0
TOTALS	9	96	30	1

INTERCEPTIONS	NO.	YDS.	LG.	TD
Blount	1	10	10	0
Greene	1	10	10	0
Wagner	1	26	26	0
TOTALS	3	46	26	0

MINNESOTA VIKINGS

RUSHING	ATT.	NET YDS.	AVG.	LONG GAIN	TD
Osborn	8	−1	−0.1	2	0
Foreman	12	18	1.5	12	0
Tarkenton	1	0	0.0	0	0
TOTALS	21	17	0.8	12	0

PASSING	ATT.	COMP.	YDS.	TKD	YDS.	TD	LG.	Had Int.
Tarkenton	26	11	102	0	0	0	28	3
TOTALS	26	11	102	0	0	0	28	3

PASS RECEIVING	NO.	YDS.	LG.	TD
Gilliam	1	16	16	0
Osborn	2	7	4	0
Foreman	5	50	17	0
Voigt	2	31	28	0
Reed	1	−2	−2	0
TOTALS	11	102	28	0

INTERCEPTIONS	NO.	YDS.	LG.	TD
TOTALS	0	0	0	0

Pittsburgh Steelers

PUNTING	NO.	YDS.	AVG.	LG.	TD
Walden	7	243	34.7	52	0
TOTALS	7	243	34.7	52	0

PUNT RETURNS	NO.	FC	YDS.	LG.	TD
Swann	3	0	34	17	0
Edwards	2	0	2	2	0
TOTALS	5	0	36	17	0

KICKOFF RETURNS	NO.	YDS.	LG.	TD
Pearson	1	15	15	0
Harrison	2	17	17	0
TOTALS	3	32	17	0

FUMBLES	Fum.	Own Rec.	Yds.	TD	Opp. Rec.	Yds.	TD	Out Bds.
Walden	1	1	-7	0	0	0	0	0
Bleier	1	0	0	0	0	0	0	0
Kellum	0	0	0	0	1	0	0	0
Harris	2	1	0	0	0	0	0	0
Greene	0	0	0	0	1	0	0	0
TOTALS 4		2	-7	0	2	0	0	0

Minnesota Vikings

PUNTING	NO.	YDS.	AVG.	LG.	TD
Eischeid	6	223	37.2	42	0
TOTALS	6	223	37.2	42	0

PUNT RETURNS	No.	FC	YDS.	LG.	TD
McCullum	3	0	11	6	0
N. Wright	1	0	1	1	0
Wallace	0	1	0	0	0
TOTALS	4	1	12	6	0

KICKOFF RETURNS	NO.	YDS.	LG.	TD
B. Brown	1	2	2	0
McCullum	1	26	26	0
McClanahan	1	22	22	0
TOTALS	3	50	26	0

FUMBLES	Fum.	Own Rec.	Yds.	TD	Opp. Rec.	Yds.	TD	Out Bds.
Poltl	0	0	0	0	1	0	0	0
Tarkenton	1	1	-10	0	0	0	0	0
B. Brown	1	0	0	0	0	0	0	0
Krause	0	0	0	0	1	0	0	0
Foreman	1	0	0	0	0	0	0	0
TOTALS 3		1	-10	0	2	0	0	0

FINAL TEAM STATISTICS

	PITTSBURGH	MINNESOTA
Total First Downs	17	9
First downs rushing	11	2
First downs passing	5	5
First downs by penalty	1	2
Third Down Efficiency	7—18	5—12
Total Offensive Yardage	333	119
Total no. offensive plays		
(Inc. times thrown passing)	73	47
Average gain per offensive play	4.6	2.5
Net Rushing Yardage	249	17
Total rushing plays	57	21
Average gain per rushing play	4.4	0.8
Net Passing Yardage	84	102
Gross yards gained passing	96	102
Times thrown and yards lost attempting		
to pass	2—12	0—0
Passes Attempted—Completed—Had Intercepted	14—9—0	26—11—3
Average gain per pass play		
(Inc. times thrown passing)	5.3	3.9
Punts—Number and Average	7—34.7	6—37.2
Had blocked	1	0
Fumbles—Number and Lost	4—2	3—2
Penalties—Number and Yards	8—122	4—18
Total Return Yardage	114	62
No. and yards punt returns	5—36	4—12
No. and yards kickoff returns	3—32	3—50
No. and yards interception returns	3—46	0—0
No. and yards miscellaneous returns		
(Field goals and blocked punts)	0	0

DEFENSIVE STATISTICS

PITTSBURGH STEELERS	Tackles	Assists	Fumble Recovery	Pass Defensed	Pass Intercepted	Punt, FG, PAT Blocked	Tackled Passer
22 Conn							
23 Wagner	2	1		1	1		
24 Thomas	3			2			
27 Edwards	1			1			
31 Shell	1						
34 Russell	4			2			
38 Bradley	3						
45 Allen	1						
47 Blount	1	1			1		
51 Toews	2						
54 Kellum	1		1				
58 Lambert	4	2		2			
59 Ham	2						
62 Wolf							
63 Holmes	4			1			
64 Furness							
68 Greenwood	2	1		3			
75 Greene	1		1		1		
77 C. Davis							
78 White	3						
86 Garrett	1						

MINNESOTA VIKINGS	Tackles	Assists	Fumble Recovery	Pass Defensed	Pass Intercepted	Punt, FG, PAT Blocked	Tackled Passer
21 Blanak							
22 Krause	5	2	1				
23 J. Wright	2	6					
24 Brown, T.				1			
25 Wallace	4	1		4			
29 Poltl	1		1				
43 N. Wright							
50 Siemon	10	5					
54 McNeill							
55 Martin	1						
58 Hilgenberg	6	1					
59 Blair	2					1	
60 Winston	6	6					
69 Sutherland	6	6					
70 Marshall	4	1					
71 Boone							
75 Lurtsema	1	1					1
77 Larsen	1						
81 Eller	7	1					
88 Page	9	1					1
89 Kingsriter	1						
53 Tingelhoff	1						
33 McClanahan	1						
73 Yary	1						

THE 1974 STEELERS — GAME BY GAME

PITTSBURGH 30, BALTIMORE 0—At Three Rivers Stadium, attendance 48,890. Joe Gilliam, starting at QB after leading the Steelers to the only perfect preseason record in the NFL, 6-0, threw TD passes to rookie Lynn Swann and Frank Lewis and completed 17 of 31 for 257 yards. It was the first shutout for the Steelers since Dec. 3, 1972, and their 15th victory in 16 regular season starts at home. Colt QBs Marty Domres and Bert Jones were sacked six times, Domres suffering bruised ribs and shoulder in the second quarter. Yogi Berra's son, Tim, recovered a fumble for the Colts in his pro debut.

Baltimore	0	0	0	0 — 0
Pittsburgh	3	13	7	7 — 30

Pitt—FG Gerela 31; Pitt—Swann 54, pass from Gilliam (kick failed); Pitt—Lewis 4 pass from Gilliam (Gerela kick); Pitt—Harris 4 run (Gerela kick); Pitt—Fuqua 4 run (Gerela kick)

PITTSBURGH 35, DENVER 35 (tie)—At Mile High Stadium, attendance 51,068. The NFL's first regular season overtime game ended in a tie after 60 minutes of regulation play and 15 minutes of "sudden death." The Broncos led 21-7 at the end of the first quarter, but Joe Gilliam, who completed 31 of 50 passes for 348 yards and 1 TD, brought them back. Barney Chavous and Bill Thompson blocked a Pittsburgh 25-yard FG try by Roy Gerela with five seconds left in regulation time. John Rowser, former Steeler, stopped a Pittsburgh overtime drive with an interception, and Jim Turner's 41-yard FG try was wide with 3:13 to go in the extra period. The game lasted 3 hours 49 minutes with 160 plays, 93 by the Steelers. Denver's Otis Armstrong topped the rushers with 131 yards and added 86 as a pass receiver.

Pittsburgh	7	7	14	7	0 — 35
Denver	21	0	7	7	0 — 35

Den—Armstrong 45 pass from Johnson (Turner kick); Pit—Davis 61 pass from Gilliam (Gerela kick); Den—Moses 7 pass from Johnson (Turner kick); Den—Keyworth 1 run (Turner kick); Pit—Gilliam 1 run (Gerela kick); Pit—Steve Davis 1 run (Gerela kick); Den—Odoms 3 pass from Ramsey (Turner kick); Pit—Steve Davis 1 run (Gerela kick); Pit—Fuqua 1 run (Gerela kick); Den—Armstrong 23 pass from Ramsey (Turner kick)

OAKLAND 17, PITTSBURGH 0—At Three Rivers Stadium, attendance 48,304. The Raiders shut out the Steelers for the first time since Nov. 15, 1964, ending a 132-game scoring string, by limiting Joe Gilliam to eight completions in 31 attempts, intercepting three times, and recovering one fumble. The Raiders also sacked Gilliam twice. Ron Smith's punt returns of 47 and 26 yards led to Ken Stabler's touchdown and his scoring pass to Cliff Branch. A George Blanda FG late in the second quarter ended the scoring for the day.

Oakland	7	10	0	0 — 17
Pittsburgh	0	0	0	0 — 0

Oak—Stabler 1 run (Blanda kick); Oak—Branch 19 pass from Stabler (Blanda kick); Oak—FG Blanda 25.

PITTSBURGH 13, HOUSTON 7—At the Astrodome, attendance 30,049. Preston Pearson came off the bench and ran for 117 yards in 15 carries, scoring the winning touchdown after Roy Gerela kicked two field goals. Billy Johnson, Houston's quick little rookie from Widener, raced 47 yards for a score on an end-around play. The Oilers lost scoring chances on penalties, two fumbles and an interception. Jim Gilliam passed for 202 yards but was intercepted twice by safety Tommy Maxwell.

Pittsburgh	0	3	3	7 — 13
Houston	0	7	0	0 — 7

Hou—B. Johnson 47 run (Butler kick); Pit—FG Gerela 37; Pit—FG Gerela 27; Pit—Pearson 9 run (Gerela kick)

PITTSBURGH 34, KANSAS CITY 24—At Arrowhead, attendance 65,517. Seven interceptions and two fumble recoveries helped Pittsburgh turn back Kansas City despite three touchdown passes by Mike Livingston. The Chiefs' three quarterbacks threw 49 passes, a club record, and completed only 16. Glen Edwards, Jack Ham and Jack Lambert each picked off two passes and the Steelers sacked Livingston three times. Joe Gilliam was on target at key stages, completing 14 of 36 for 214 yards and one touchdown. The Chiefs led twice in the early stages but were able to make only 58 yards rushing.

Pittsburgh	7	17	10	0 — 34
Kansas City	3	7	7	7 — 24

KC—FG Stenerud 31; Pit—Bleier 2 run (Gerela kick); KC—P. Pearson 13 pass from Livingston (Stenerud kick); Pit—B. Pearson 3 run (Gerela kick); Pit—Edwards 49 interception return (Gerela kick); Pit—FG Gerela 32; KC—Taylor 10 pass from Livingston (Stenerud kick); Pit—FG Gerela 45; Pit—Lewis 31 pass from Gilliam (Gerela kick); KC—Wright 13 pass from Livingston (Stenerud kick)

PITTSBURGH 20, CLEVELAND 16—At Three Rivers Stadium, attendance 48,100. Roy Gerela kicked two decisive field goals despite a leg injury and Glen Edwards picked off a desperation fourth-down pass by Mike Phipps in the final minute to save a Pittsburgh victory. Joe Gilliam completed only five of 18 passes for a net 66 yards against the aroused Browns. The Steelers sacked Phipps six times for 33 yards. Franco Harris rushed for 81 yards and one touchdown on 14 carries.

Cleveland	0	13	0	3 — 16
Pittsburgh	7	7	3	3 — 20

Pit—Pearson 6 run (Gerela kick); Pit—Harris 1 run (Gerela kick); Cle—Phipps 18 run (Cockroft kick); Cle—Morin 9 pass from Phipps (kick blocked); Pit—FG Gerela 31; Cle—FG Cockroft 21; Pit—FG Gerela 26

PITTSBURGH 24, ATLANTA 17—At Three Rivers Stadium, attendance 48,094. Franco Harris set a career high of 141 yards and Rocky Bleier ran for 78 as Terry Bradshaw returned to his old starting quarterback job for the Steelers in a Monday night game. Bradshaw also scored once. The Steelers sacked Bob Lee seven times, boosting their league-leading total to 28, but Lee completed touchdown passes to Al Dodd and Ken Burrow to keep it close. L. C. Greenwood had three sacks.

Atlanta	0	14	0	3 — 17
Pittsburgh	14	0	3	7 — 24

Pit—Bleier 10 run (Gerela kick); Pit—Bradshaw 1 run (Gerela kick); Atl—Dodd 9 pass from Lee (Mike-Mayer kick); Atl—Burrow 24 pass from Lee (Mike-Mayer kick); Pit—FG Gerela 33; Pit—Harris 7 run (Gerela kick); Atl—FG Mike-Mayer 32

PITTSBURGH 27, PHILADELPHIA 0—At Three Rivers Stadium, attendance 47,996. Pittsburgh won its seventh straight over NFC opposition and scored its second shutout of the year at the expense of the Eagles who were held to 143 yards. Terry Bradshaw directed a 375-yard offense, threw a touchdown pass and gained 48 yards rushing as the Steelers maintained their 1½-game lead in the AFC

Central. Pittsburgh increased its league-leading total of sacks to 32 by dumping Philadelphia quarterbacks four times and also intercepted two passes. Franco Harris led the parade with 70 yards.

Philadelphia	0	0	0	0 — 0
Pittsburgh	7	10	10	0 — 27

Pitt—Lewis 8 pass from Bradshaw (Gerela kick); Pitt—Harris 5 run (Gerela kick); Pitt—FG Gerela 35; Pitt—FG Gerela 28; Pitt—Blount 52 interception return (Gerela kick)

CINCINNATI 17, PITTSBURGH 10—At Riverfront Stadium, attendance 57,532. Ken Anderson completed 20 of 22 passes and broke two NFL records, and then made a game-saving tackle to move the Bengals within a half game of the leading Steelers in the AFC Central Division. Anderson went into the game with a string of eight consecutive completions and increased the total to 16, topping the league record set by Len Dawson in 1967 and equaled by Joe Namath the same year. Anderson's 90.9 percentage for his 20-of-22 topped the record of 86-21 set by Stabler last year with 25-of-29. Doug Dressler caught 9 passes and sub Ed Williams scored two touchdowns.

Pittsburgh	0	3	0	7 — 10
Cincinnati	0	10	7	0 — 17

Cin—Williams 2 run (Muhlmann kick); Cin—FG Muhlmann 30; Pitt—FG Gerela 24; Cin—Williams 1 run (Muhlmann kick); Pitt—Pearson 1 run (Gerela kick)

PITTSBURGH 26, CLEVELAND 16—At Cleveland Stadium, attendance 77,739. Franco Harris gained 156 yards on 23 carries and Roy Gerela booted four field goals to help the Steelers widen their AFC Central lead to 1½ games with a victory over the Browns. There were 13 turnovers, including a touchdown by J. T. Thomas on a lateral from Joe Greene who recovered a Billy Lefear fumble. Terry Hanratty started his first game of the season as Pittsburgh quarterback.

Pittsburgh	7	6	0	13 — 26
Cleveland	3	3	10	0 — 16

Cle—FG Cockroft 44; Pitt—Shanklin 28 pass from Hanratty (Gerela kick); Pitt—FG Gerela 32; Cle—FG Cockroft 35; Pitt—FG Gerela 32; Cle—Greene 36 interception return (Cockroft kick); Cle—FG Cockroft 18; Pitt—FG Gerela 23; Pitt—Thomas 14 fumble recovery return (Gerela kick); Pitt—FG Gerela 22

PITTSBURGH 28, NEW ORLEANS 7—At Tulane Stadium, attendance 71,907. The Steelers, with Terry Bradshaw at quarterback again, overwhelmed the Saints and maintained their 1½-game lead over Cincinnati in the AFC Central Division. Bradshaw passed for two touchdowns and rushed for 99 yards, including an 18-yard scoring run. Franco Harris paced Pittsburgh's 272-yard ground attack, with 114 yards. The Steelers had six sacks to boost their league-leading total to 46.

Pittsburgh	7	7	14	0 — 28
New Orleans	0	0	7	0 — 7

Pitt—Lewis 31 pass from Bradshaw (Gerela kick); Pitt—Bradshaw 18 run (Gerela kick); Pitt—Swann 64 punt return (Gerela kick); NO—Seal 10 pass from Scott (McClard kick); Pitt—Brown 1 pass from Bradshaw (Gerela kick)

HOUSTON 13, PITTSBURGH 10—At Three Rivers Stadium, attendance 41,195. Houston won its fifth game in the last six starts on a 34-yard field goal by Skip Butler with 2:32 to play. The Steelers were held to 84 yards in a game played in steady, freezing rain. Dan Pastorini passed to Fred Willis for the touchdown and

Butler added two field goals. Terry Bradshaw threw one scoring pass but left the game with bruised ribs in the third quarter. The Oilers sacked Steeler quarterbacks four times and intercepted three passes, two by rookie Gregg Bingham.

Houston	0	7	3	3 — 13
Pittsburgh	3	7	0	0 — 10

Pitt—FG Gerela 44; Hou—Willis 6 pass from Pastorini (Butler kick); Pitt—Harris 31 pass from Bradshaw (Gerela kick); Hou—FG Butler 42; Hou—FG Butler 34

PITTSBURGH 21, NEW ENGLAND 17—At Schaefer Stadium, attendance 61,279. Franco Harris led Steelers to AFC Central Division championship with 136 yards on 29 carries while the Pittsburgh defense held the Patriots to 184 yards. The defeat eliminated New England from contention for a wild card berth in the playoffs. Pittsburgh had three more sacks for a league-leading total of 52, including a safety when L. C. Greenwood tackled Jim Plunkett in the end zone. Roy Gerela's two field goals kept him out front in the scoring race with 84 points.

Pittsburgh	0	12	7	2 — 21
New England	7	3	0	7 — 17

NE—Herron 17 pass from Plunkett (Smith kick); Pitt—FG Gerela 40; Pitt—Harris 2 run (kick blocked); Pitt—FG Gerela 27; NE—FG Smith 20; Pitt—Swann 7 pass from Bradshaw (Gerela kick); Pitt—Safety, Greenwood tackled Plunkett in end zone; NE—Herron 5 run (Smith kick)

PITTSBURGH 27, CINCINNATI 3—At Three Rivers Stadium, attendance 42,878. Franco Harris went over the 1,000-yard mark with 1,006 and Terry Bradshaw threw two touchdown passes as Steelers won 10th game for third straight year. The Bengals, battered by injuries, used a patchwork lineup with Wayne Clark replacing injured Ken Anderson at quarterback. Roy Gerela's two field goals and three conversions gave him the AFC scoring title with 93 points. Lynn Swann returned three punts for 112 yards for a league-leading total of 577 yards, only 35 short of the record.

Cincinnati	0	0	3	0 — 3
Pittsburgh	7	10	7	3 — 27

Pitt—Stallworth 5 pass from Bradshaw (Gerela kick); Pitt—Mullins 7 pass from Bradshaw (Gerela kick); Pitt—FG Gerela 26; Cin—FG Muhlmann 32; Pitt—Harrison 1 run (Gerela kick); Pitt—FG Gerela 42

AFC DIVISIONAL PLAYOFF

SUN., DEC 22—PITTSBURGH 32, BUFFALO 14—At Three Rivers Stadium, attendance 48,321. Franco Harris led the Steelers into their second AFC title game in three years by scoring a record three touchdowns and tied another conference divisional playoff mark with 18 points. Pittsburgh broke the game wide open with 26 points in the second quarter and rolled up 438 yards under the direction of quarterback Terry Bradshaw. Harris carried 24 times for 74 yards and Bradshaw ran for 48 yards, while O. J. Simpson of the Bills was held to 49 yards. Joe Ferguson passed for both Buffalo scores to tight end Paul Seymour and Simpson. The Steelers set a divisional playoff record with 29 first downs.

Buffalo	7	0	7	0 — 14
Pittsburgh	3	26	0	3 — 32

Pitt—FG Gerela 21; Buff—Seymour 22 pass from Ferguson (Leypoldt kick); Pitt—Bleier 27 pass from Bradshaw (kick blocked); Pitt—Harris 1 run (Gerela kick); Pitt—Harris 4 run (kick blocked); Harris 1 run (Gerela kick); Buff—Simpson 3 pass from Ferguson (Leypoldt kick); Pitt—FG Gerela 22

INDIVIDUAL STATISTICS

RUSHING

	Atts.	Yards	Avg.	Long	TDs
Harris	208	1006	4.8	54	5
Bleier	88	373	4.2	18	2
Pearson	70	317	4.5	53	4
St. Davis	71	246	3.5	22	2
Bradshaw	34	224	6.6	34	2
Fuqua	50	156	3.1	14	2
Gilliam	14	41	2.9	13	1
Harrison	6	30	5.0	15	1
Lewis	2	25	12.5	22	0
Swann	1	14	14.0	14	0
Hanratty	1	—6	—6.0	—6	0
Stallworth	1	—9	—9.0	—9	0

PASSING

	Att.	Comp.	Pct.	Yards	TDs	%TDs	Long	Int.	%Int.	Avg.
Gilliam	212	96	45.3	1274	4	1.9	61	8	3.8	6.01
Bradshaw	148	67	45.3	785	7	4.7	56	8	5.4	5.30
Hanratty	26	3	11.5	95	1	3.8	35	5	19.2	3.65

PASS RECEIVING

	No	Yards	Avg.	Long	TDs
Lewis	30	365	12.2	31	4
Harris	23	200	8.7	31	1
Shanklin	19	324	17.1	35	1
Brown	17	190	11.2	35	1
Stallworth	16	269	16.8	56	1
Grossman	13	164	12.6	32	0
Swann	11	208	18.9	54	2
St. Davis	11	152	13.8	61	1
Pearson	11	118	10.7	31	0
Bleier	7	87	12.4	24	0
Fuqua	6	68	11.3	18	0
Mullins	1	7	7.0	7	1
Harrison	1	2	2.0	2	0

INTERCEPTIONS

	No.	Yards	Long	TDs
Edwards	5	153	59	1
Thomas	5	22	14	0
Ham	5	13	10	0
Blount	2	74	52	0
Lambert	2	19	13	0
Wagner	2	13	9	0
Greene	1	26	26	0
Kellum	1	0	0	0
Russell	1	0	0	0
Shell	1	0	0	0

PUNTING

	No.	Yards	Avg.	Long	Blk.
Walden	78	3040	39.0	65	0

PUNT RETURNS

	No.	FC	Yards	Avg.	Long	TDs
Swann	41	3	577	14.1	69	1
Edwards	16	0	128	8.0	19	0
Conn	10	0	69	6.9	18	0

KICKOFF RETURNS

	No.	Yards	Avg.	Long	TDs
Conn	1	34	34.0	34	0
Blount	5	152	30.4	60	0
St. Davis	12	269	22.4	34	0
Bleier	3	67	22.3	35	0
Pearson	12	258	21.5	29	0
Harrison	4	72	18.0	27	0
Edwards	2	31	15.5	19	0
Allen	1	7	7.0	7	0
Swann	2	11	5.5	11	0

SCORING

	TDs	Rush.	Rec.	Ret.	XP	XPA	FG	FGA	S	Points
Gerela	0	0	0	0	33	35	20	29	0	93
Harris	6	5	1	0	0	0	0	0	0	36
Lewis	4	0	4	0	0	0	0	0	0	24
Pearson	4	4	0	0	0	0	0	0	0	24
St. Davis	3	2	1	0	0	0	0	0	0	18
Swann	3	0	2	1	0	0	0	0	0	18
Bleier	2	2	0	0	0	0	0	0	0	12
Bradshaw	2	2	0	0	0	0	0	0	0	12
Fuqua	2	2	0	0	0	0	0	0	0	12
Blount	1	0	0	1	0	0	0	0	0	6
Brown	1	0	1	0	0	0	0	0	0	6
Edwards	1	0	0	1	0	0	0	0	0	6
Gilliam	1	1	0	0	0	0	0	0	0	6
Harrison	1	1	0	0	0	0	0	0	0	6
Mullins	1	0	1	0	0	0	0	0	0	6
Shanklin	1	0	1	0	0	0	0	0	0	6
Stallworth	1	0	1	0	0	0	0	0	0	6
Thomas	1	0	0	1	0	0	0	0	0	6
Greenwood	0	0	0	0	0	0	0	0	1	2

FINAL 1974 NFL TEAM STANDING

AMERICAN CONFERENCE

Eastern Division

	W	L	T	Pct.	Pts.	OP
Miami	11	3	0	.786	327	216
Buffalo	9	5	0	.643	264	244
New England	7	7	0	.500	348	289
New York	7	7	0	.500	279	300
Baltimore	2	12	0	.143	190	329

Central Division

	W	L	T	Pct.	Pts.	OP
PITTSBURGH	10	3	1	.750	305	189
Cincimoti	7	7	0	.500	283	259
Houston	7	7	0	.500	236	282
Cleveland	4	10	0	.286	251	344

Western Division

	W	L	T	Pct.	Pts.	OP
Oakland	12	2	0	.857	355	228
Denver	7	6	1	.536	302	294
Kansas City	5	9	0	.357	233	293
San Diego	5	9	0	.357	212	285

AFC Playoffs
PITTSBURGH 32, Buffalo 14
Oakland 28, Miami 26

AFC Championship
PITTSBURGH 24, Oakland 13

NATIONAL CONFERENCE

Eastern Division

	W	L	T	Pct.	Pts.	OP
St. Louis	10	4	0	.714	285	218
Washington	10	4	0	.714	320	196
Dallas	8	6	0	.571	297	235
Philadelphia	7	7	0	.500	242	217
New York Giants	2	12	0	.143	195	299

Central Division

	W	L	T	Pct.	Pts.	OP
Minnesota	10	4	0	.714	310	195
Detroit	7	7	0	.500	256	270
Green Bay	6	8	0	.429	210	206
Chicago	4	10	0	.286	152	279

Western Division

	W	L	T	Pct.	Pts.	OP
Los Angeles	10	4	0	.714	263	181
San Francisco	6	8	0	.429	226	236
New Orleans	5	9	0	.357	166	263
Atlanta	3	11	0	.214	111	271

NFC Playoffs
Minnesota 30, St. Louis 14
Los Angeles 19, Washington 10

NFC Championship
Minnesota 14, Los Angeles 10

SUPER BOWL IX
PITTSBURGH 16, Minnesota 6

STEELERS 1974 SCORES AND ATTENDANCE

PRESEASON

Aug. 3 — Steelers 26 @ New Orleans	7	45,339
Aug. 12 — Steelers 50 — Chicago	21	42,325
Aug. 17 — Steelers 33 @ Philadelphia	30	25,002
Aug. 24 — Steelers 17 — N. Y. Giants	7	50,056
Aug. 30 — Steelers 21 @ Washington	19	42,237
Sept. 5 — Steelers 41 @ Dallas	15	41,321

Won 6, Lost 0

Attendance: 246,270—Home: 92,381; Away: 153,889

REGULAR SEASON

Sept. 15 — Steelers 30 — Baltimore	0	48,890
Sept. 22 — Steelers 35 @ Denver	35*	51,068
Sept. 29 — Steelers 0 — Oakland	17	48,304
Oct. 6 — Steelers 13 @ Houston	7	30,049
Oct. 13 — Steelers 34 @ Kansas City	24	65,517
Oct. 20 — Steelers 20 — Cleveland	16	48,100
Oct. 28 — Steelers 24 — Atlanta	17	48,094
Nov. 3 — Steelers 27 — Philadelphia	0	47,996
Nov. 10 — Steelers 10 @ Cincinnati	17	57,532
Nov. 17 — Steelers 26 @ Cleveland	16	77,739
Nov. 25 — Steelers 28 @ New Orleans	7	71,907
Dec. 1 — Steelers 10 — Houston	13	41,195
Dec. 8 — Steelers 21 @ New England	17	52,107
Dec. 14 — Steelers 27 — Cincinnati	3	42,878

*Sudden Death

Won 10, Lost 3, Tied 1

Attendance: 731,376—Home: 325,457; Away: 405,919

POST SEASON

Dec. 22 — Steelers 32 — Buffalo	14	48,321
Dec. 29 — Steelers 24 @ Oakland	13	53,515
Jan. 12 — Steelers 16 — Minnesota	6	80,997

Attendance: 182,824

STEELERS 1974 INDIVIDUAL HONORS

MEL BLOUNT—
  All AFC Honorable Mention—UPI

ROY GERELA—
  All NFL 2nd team—AP, NEA, PFWA
  All AFC 1st team—AP, Sporting News, UPI
  Pro Bowl—2nd time

JOE GREENE
  All NFL 1st team—AP, NEA, PFW, PFWA
  All AFC 1st team—AP, PFW, Sporting News, UPI
  Pro Bowl—6th time
  NFL—Most Valuable Defensive Player—AP

L. C. GREENWOOD—
  All NFL 1st team—AP, PFWA
  All NFL 2nd team—NEA
  All AFC 1st team—AP, PFW, Sporting News, AP
  Pro Bowl—2nd time

JACK HAM—
  All NFL 1st team—AP, NEA, PFW, PFWA
  All AFC 1st team—AP, PFW, Sporting News, UPI
  Pro Bowl—2nd time

FRANCO HARRIS—
  All AFC 2nd team—UPI
  Pro Bowl—3rd time
  Most Valuable Player—Super Bowl

ERNIE HOLMES—
  All NFL 2nd team—NEA
  All AFC Honorable Mention—UPI

JON KOLB—
  All AFC 2nd team—UPI

JACK LAMBERT—
  All AFC Honorable Mention—AP
  All NFL Rookie team—PFW, PFWA, UPI
  NFL Defensive Rookie of the Year—AP

RAY MANSFIELD—
  All AFC Honorable Mention—AP

ANDY RUSSELL—
  All AFC 1st team—PFW
  All AFC 2nd team—UPI
  Pro Bowl—6th time

LYNN SWANN—
  All NFL Rookie team—PFWA

MIKE WEBSTER—
  All NFL Rookie team—PFW, PFWA

DWIGHT WHITE—
  All AFC 2nd team—UPI

STEELER TEAM RECORDS SET IN 1974
Season
Fewest Net Yards Gained by Opponents—3,074 yards
Fewest Net Yards Gained Passing by Opponents—1,466 yards
Fewest Passes Completed by Opponents—141 (14 game season)
Fewest Passes Completed—147 (14 game season)
Most Punts by Opponents—91
Most Punt Returns—67
Most Yardage by Punt Returns—774
Most Penalties—104
Most Penalty Yards—978
Most Quarterback Sacks—52
Most First Downs by Penalties by Opponents—30

Game
Most Passes Completed—31 (9-22-74 vs. Denver)

STEELERS TEAM RECORDS TIED IN 1974
Game
Most Touchdowns Rushing—4 (9-22-74 vs. Denver)
Most Field Goals—4 (11-17-74 vs. Cleveland)
Fewest Passes Attempted by Opponents—8 (12-14-74 vs. Cincinnati)

STEELERS INDIVIDUAL RECORDS SET IN 1974
Career
Most Total Points—413 Roy Gerela (1971-74)
Most Field Goals—94 Roy Gerela (1971-74)
Most Textra Points—131 Roy Gerela (1971-74)
Most Extra Points—135 Roy Gerela (1971-74)
Most Punts—504 Bobby Walden (1968-74)
Most Punt Returns—73 Glen Edwards (1971-74)

Season
Most Punt Returns—41 Lynn Swann
Most Yards Punt Returns—577 Lynn Swann

Game
Most Passes Attempted—50 Joe Gilliam (9-22-75 ve. Denver)
Most Passes Completed—31 Joe Gilliam (9-22-75 vs. Denver)

SUPER BOWL TEAM RECORDS SET BY STEELERS
Fewest Net Yards Gained by Opponents—119
Fewest Yards Gained Rushing by Opponents—17
Most Rushing Attempts—57
Most Yards Gained by Punt Returns—36

SUPER BOWL INDIVIDUAL RECORDS SET BY STEELERS
Most Yards Gained Rushing—158, Franco Harris
Most Rushing Attempts—34, Franco Harris
Highest Punt Return Average—11.3, Lynn Swann